PTS ME

Trauma, Triumph, and Survival of a Small Town Cop

BY: D.T. Hudson

©2019 dthudsonllc, TX-8-732-456, April 2019
All rights reserved. No part of this publication may reproduced, distributed, or transmitted in any form or by any means, including photocopying, recording or other Electronic or mechanical methods, without the prior written permission of the author except in the case of brief quotations embodied in critical reviews and certain other noncommercial used permitted by copyright law.

<u>Disclaimer</u>

The views and contents in this book do not necessarily represent the views of any specific agency or the United States.

"Whoever fights monsters should see to it that in the process that he does not become a monster. For when you look long into an abyss, the abyss also looks into you".
Nietzsche

CONTENTS

<u>*Foreword*</u>

The Mayo Clinic describes Post-Traumatic Stress Disorder (PTSD) as a mental health condition that's triggered by a terrifying event — either experiencing it or witnessing it. Symptoms may include flashbacks, nightmares and severe anxiety, as well as uncontrollable thoughts about the event.

Most people who go through traumatic events may have temporary difficulty adjusting and coping, but with time and good self-care, they usually get better. If the symptoms get worse, last for months or even years, and interfere with your day-to-day functioning, you may have PTSD.

Post-traumatic stress disorder symptoms may start within one month of a traumatic event, but sometimes symptoms may not appear until years after the event. These symptoms can cause significant problems in social or work situations and in relationships. They can also interfere with your ability to go about your normal daily tasks.

PTSD symptoms are generally grouped into four types: intrusive memories, avoidance, negative changes in thinking and mood, and changes in physical and emotional reactions. Symptoms can vary over time or vary from person to person.

Intrusive memories

Symptoms of intrusive memories may include:

- Recurrent, unwanted distressing memories of the traumatic event

- Reliving the traumatic event as if it were happening again (flashbacks)

- Upsetting dreams or nightmares about the traumatic event

- Severe emotional distress or physical reactions to something that reminds you of the traumatic event

Avoidance

Symptoms of avoidance may include:

- Trying to avoid thinking or talking about the traumatic event

- Avoiding places, activities or people that remind you of the traumatic event

Negative changes in thinking and mood

Symptoms of negative changes in thinking and mood may include:

- Negative thoughts about yourself, other people or the world

- Hopelessness about the future

- Memory problems, including not remembering important aspects of the traumatic event

- Difficulty maintaining close relationships

- Feeling detached from family and friends

- Lack of interest in activities you once enjoyed

- Difficulty experiencing positive emotions

- Feeling emotionally numb

Changes in physical and emotional reactions

Symptoms of changes in physical and emotional reactions (also called arousal symptoms) may include:

- Being easily startled or frightened

- Always being on guard for danger

- Self-destructive behavior, such as drinking too much or driving too fast

- Trouble sleeping

- Trouble concentrating

- Irritability, angry outbursts or aggressive behavior

- Overwhelming guilt or shame

Intensity of symptoms

PTSD symptoms can vary in intensity over time. You may have more PTSD symptoms when you're stressed in general, or when you come across reminders of what you went through. For example, you may hear a car backfire and relive combat experiences. Or you may see a report on the news about a sexual assault and feel overcome by memories of your own assault.

When to see a doctor

If you have disturbing thoughts and feelings about a traumatic event for more than a month, if they're severe, or if you feel you're having trouble getting your life back under control, talk to your doctor or a mental health professional. Getting treatment as soon as possible can help prevent PTSD symptoms from getting worse.

*Patient Care and Health Information, Diseases and Condition, Post-traumatic Stress Disorder (PTSD). (2018, July 18). Retrieved from https://www.mayoclinic.org/diseases-conditions/post-traumatic-stress-disorder/symptoms-causes/syc-20355967.In text: ("Post-traumatic Stress Disorder (PTSD)", 2018)

Prologue

I believe that the first step of a successful life is a foundation that is strong and able to withstand the changes unexpectedly thrown at us. Without a strong foundation, the integrity of everything it built upon is compromised. In short, if you build your house in a mud puddle, expect to get wet.

Even possessing a fairly firm foundation, I have regrets - many of them. Some professional. Some personal. One regret that I wanted to avoid, however, was missing the opportunity to tell the following stories. Hoping in the telling, I can help others who may be struggling with their own regrets.

When I started this project, it was my intent to collect stories from my friends and colleagues. I certainly did not want this book to be about just me. There is so much more in this world than my story. Initially, I decided to solicit experiences from my colleagues. Querying these people produced an overwhelming and positive response to the idea of this book. It seemed there would be no lack of material relating to experiences in the emergency services professions, regardless of their location. Everyone I spoke with was excited to share some experience. After initial contact, I waited and waited for these stories to come flowing to me in written form.

Instead of an endless trail of stories and material, I received nothing.

At first, I was very confused. I had received such an overwhelming response and support from my colleagues when I contacted them about the project, but where were *their* stories?

Giving much thought to the discordance between telling a story amongst colleagues and being willing to share a story with a wider audience, a light bulb turned on in my head. Perhaps the lack of material was because, unlike my colleagues, I had already started a journey toward facing these memories, and others had not yet left the starting line.

As I write today, I have learned an important lesson: Reliving one event, positive or negative, can uncontrollably bring memories of other events to your conscious mind. These other events may not even be related to a profession. (It happens in our personal lives too.) Even though my colleagues loved the idea of this book and wanted to share their own stories, that very stimulus of recalling a memory perhaps caused other memories to come alive. Memories that had been previously stored safely, deep inside. Those deep memories are not easy to revisit or to share. This was so true for me until one amazing day.

What I decided next was to humbly put myself out there. My hope is that a colleague reading this may be able to relate and understand what is happening or has happened to his or her own life. I also hope that the general public will have a greater understanding and perhaps even compassion for those who have devoted their lives to helping others.

After conversations with some colleagues, one brave solider shared his story. He experienced horror that most of us would avoid. That horror continues to follow him today. Much to this hero's credit, he has found solutions through his own group. His need to protect his fellow soldiers and family has never left. To his credit, he realized that his story may just do that, protect those whom he cares the most. This hero not only wanted to share his story, he has made it a goal to encourage other people to share their stories. The therapy of writing, actually thinking about what you are writing, and then reading it over and over again is similar to Prolonged Exposure Therapy. Memories forgotten appearing, making apparent the clutter that entangles us in our daily lives. I commend this soldier as he continues to be a warrior and champion for those living in their own personal hell.

I was contacted by a former colleague. He also expressed a desire to share some of his stories. I was enlightened after reading the soldier and my former colleague's stories. To my amazement, these two individuals could not be more opposite, but their struggles and mine, are so much the same. I cannot help but think there are more people out there with the same struggle. So many in fact, it would warrant their own book, with their own stories. I can only assume our stories may help even that one person. I guess my goal will then be achieved.

I am not a doctor, therapist, or lawyer. I am a cop that had some uncontrollable experiences that affected my life in many ways. I was reluctant to tell my story, as it is just that, my story. But I hope you find it interesting. I hope if you feel your own experiences in life have changed you in a negative way, or you feel an unwanted void in your life, this may help guide you to those that can help you find your answers. My goal, regardless of who you are or what you have experienced, is that someday you may want to share your story with me and others.

The purpose of telling these stories is to make you laugh, cry, and to help you understand the subculture of these not-so–every-day- people in emergency and public service. The story doesn't end after each individual experience. There are profound effects that last a lifetime. These effects have been often misunderstood, ignored, or whisked away by bravado and fear by those who have experienced them. I felt the same way until I learned what was happening to me. I proudly come from the ranks of these public servants.

I don't claim to see, feel, or speak for anyone in these stories other than my own recollection. Many of these stories were reported by local and national media. I do not profess to know all the facts other than what I experienced, observed, remember and reported. Some are clear and vivid, others took years to explore and understand.

Even though my goal is to present examples in my life that are reflective of the adversities and dangers experienced by others in emergency and public service, I have found that many of the most tragic and frightening stories cannot be shared due to the sensitivity of the situations and out of respect to the victims. I hope, though, that these examples can serve as a catalyst toward understanding by the public and as a sign of comradery to my sisters and brothers who may be struggling with their own stories but are fearful to share with others.

I don't have answers, just my experiences and how this path transformed me, good and bad. This book will give you no medical or legal advice. It's just me, a couple of dear friends, and maybe it is you too. If it is you, please reach out. You have many brothers and sisters out there who understand and have similar stories.

My intent is not to give away tactics, secret information, or other training used by law enforcement. Some of the information regarding names, places, dates, and techniques is intentionally vague. It is important that specific information regarding these items be kept vague for safety reasons. You see, life goes on. There is still the cop on the beat and the agent or detective planning their next warrant. This is simply my story, from beginning to present.

<u>**Part I**</u>

<u>**The Boy**</u>

<u>**You Have to Start Somewhere**</u>

Growing up in rural North Dakota has more advantages than people think. Sheltered from politics and big city crime, I was protected by a moral barrier that filtered out much of what was wrong in the world. It afforded me the opportunity to play sports, have personal relationships, responsibility, and to entertain myself.

Winters can be harsh in North Dakota, but like many old-school Norwegians say, "Uff-dah it's cold, but it keeps da riff raff out". A hearty "Ya, you betcha!" is a common response. Indeed, it does get cold, but like a chapter in a book, the weather is only part of the whole story.

I wouldn't have called myself an ignorant young man. I was more sheltered, perhaps more naïve, than anything. A church-going, God-fearing, flag-loving patriot of a boy that couldn't fathom what he would watched on the evening news. To me, those news stories were just that – stories, not real events happening somewhere else in the country or world.

As a teenager, I carried a knife every day and had a 30-06 hanging in the back window of my pick-up truck that was parked in the school parking lot. My truck was complemented by the other twenty vehicles in the same school parking lot with just as much fire power. We didn't do this to stop what is now coined "Active Shooters". We hunted before and after school.

I am the son of a hardworking farmer and a nurse that made the sacrifice to stay home and support the farm while raising their children. We were fortunate to always have food on the table and our parents at home. It was a short drive of 10 miles to any of my friend's homes. I am lucky to still have both of my parents, a brother, and a sister in my life.

As I look back, this way of life made it much simpler to be happy. Granted there were tragedies, sadness, deaths, turmoil, but a community like the one I grew up in was an extended family. They looked out for one another and were generally concerned. There is no perfect place on earth, and this was not either, but it is part of my life and I would not trade the lessons, good and bad, I learned growing up in rural North Dakota.

I never planned to stay on the farm. I didn't try and hide that I did not have an interest in farming nor did I have what it takes to be a successful farmer. As the middle child, I was a bit less reclusive than my siblings. I was looking forward to life's adventures and was excited to find what life had in store. Like a lot of young adults that come from small rural areas, life can be a bigger bite than expected. Luckily for me, I had one heck of an appetite.

I have been called many things in my life: asshole, prick, brother, son, husband, dad, just to name a few. Eventually I was called "officer". I chose law enforcement as my profession out of sheer laziness. In college I was a banking and financial services major until I joined the military in 1993. When I returned from my technical training, I asked my advisor what career or degree I had the most credits towards, because that is the major I would choose. "Sociology" I was told. At this point the mystery of which career to choose was solved.

Soon after graduating, I quickly learned that I needed to lose my cocky and lazy attitude if I was going to succeed in a career of law enforcement. In 1996, I landed my first cop job as an unpaid, part-time deputy working at special events and in the jail. Between working loss prevention, guard drills, and going to the police academy to be a full-time officer, money was tight and the future was unknown.

After a grueling series of tests and panel interviews, I eventually became a patrol officer for the Fargo Police Department in Fargo, North Dakota. Before I knew it, I had successfully completed the field training program and my one-year probationary period. During this time, I had seen my first dead body, chased people down on foot, and testified in court. I knew it all, or so I thought. I was a one-year "veteran" of the largest police department in North Dakota. This career I had chosen became more than a job. I lived, breathed, and focused on every aspect of law enforcement because I really thought I had found a home. The people I worked with on a daily basis were nothing short of extraordinary. I was an adult now, with incredible responsibilities. My career had just begun. I had no idea how much this was about to change my life forever, but more about that later.

Growing

I was one of the fortunate kids to have at least one parent home all of the time. Without that support, my story would be very different. More of a vagabond than the rest of my family, my adventurous demeanor would lead me to interesting things. Close calls were just considered the cost of being adventurous.

During my younger years, our farm had two homes situated about fifty yards apart. We had our house, and grandpa and grandma on my father's side had their home. Dad and Grandpa farmed together. As time went on, Grandpa and Grandma decided to move to town. Grandpa would continue to farm, but would commute the short seven miles west. They purchased a lot and built a rambler-style home. We sold our home to some neighbors and moved into Grandpa and

Grandma's old house. House movers lifted up our blue two-story house, and just like that, the first part of my life literally left the driveway on a trailer pulled by a truck.

Settled into our new home, I no longer shared a room with my brother. I was seven years old and enjoyed my own space. It felt like everything was falling into place in my life. I had my own space and I even had a dog named Clover. He was a mean little elkhound with a tail similar to a scorpion. Clover hated two things in life, cats and bad weather. When bad weather was inevitable, the first sound of thunder would send him tearing southbound to his safe space under an overturned aluminum boat. I cannot imagine how loud it must have sounded underneath that boat.

Living on the plains of North Dakota, you can see for miles. Watching and listening to the sky becomes an important part of growing up here and you become tuned into Mother Nature at a young age. According to meteorological statistics, the location of our farm was in the path of an unusually large number of aggressive storms. These storms often have the ability to create deadly lighting, damaging hail, and tornados.

In the summer of 1980 I was seven years old. It was a hot and humid day and our central air unit hummed away without a break. Like a painting in the sky, clouds began to organize themselves into various shapes. These shapes began to merge together into larger, darker shapes. It was hypnotic watching Mother Nature paint this picture in the sky. The wind blew the sticky air in wavy holograms of sunlight.

My father was working a field some distance away. The radio in our kitchen was on, playing the local station. A series of familiar beeps chimed as the announcer said that our area may be in for some bad weather in the next hour or so. This announcement happened so many times that rarely did any of us pay attention. Shortly after the announcement, the sun started to fade, which was odd considering it was still afternoon in the middle of summer. I could hear radio traffic from our business band radio. This radio system allowed us to communicate via radio with one another regardless of which field my father or grandfather was working. Our trucks and tractors had radios and the base station was located in the office area of our home. I heard dad say something about the weather and that he was going to be headed home.

Something felt wrong outside. The humidity had increased and the wind was now completely still. Suddenly it was difficult to breathe. Each breath felt as if Mother Nature had placed a wet wash rag over our noses and mouths. The large clouds I admired earlier had now taken on a darker, more sinister form. Lightning shot violently from all parts of the clouds.

I had been taught that a steady role of thunder typically meant hail. I could see my father making the final turn into our quarter- mile-long driveway. I was summoned back inside the house by my mother.

The radio chimed with its familiar tone and the announcer warned of severe weather. One announcement he made still baffles me, "We have a tornado sighting and severe weather announcement, but first a word from our sponsor." Whoever the sponsor was that day must have paid some big bucks.

As my father parked the tractor and made his way into the house, all hell broke loose. On the north side of our house, had many tall and narrow crank-out windows, and it got dark as night. First the wind, then the rain, followed by hail. I heard a rumble that turned into a roar. It sounded like a freight train was headed right at us. I remember seeing hail, the size of softballs, falling from the sky and bouncing off the ground.

"Everyone to the basement!" A scream broke through the weather's noise.

I don't know why but I grabbed a silver motorcycle helmet and assumed the crash position in our basement. The rest of the family also took shelter throughout the lower half of our house. Even through my helmet I could hear our house being assaulted by large hail. The sound of broken glass and the claps of thunder shook me to my core. As quickly as this hell had started, it passed. It seemed a lifetime had gone by but surely it was a matter of minutes. As we emerged from our basement, the destruction of this powerful force of nature was revealed.

The tall crank out windows were all smashed, and glass was strewn about our living room. Trees were down throughout our farm. The damage caused by the hail made tin buildings look as if some force had taken a hammer and dented them. The softball-sized hail had hit the ground with such force it caused the stones to bounce and impact our windows, shattering them. This was a mess, but it had just begun. The tornado appeared, but lifted over our farm, saving us from a much worse tragedy. The tornado wasn't done, though. It was building strength and headed right for our small hometown.

I am not a tornado survivor, more of a witness. I have seen them and know how dangerous they are. On this day, I heard and felt it. Worse yet, I saw the damage one can cause. The tornado ripped through the small town. Witnesses at the café said they saw the water sucked up like a vacuum from the swimming pool. The top of the elevator was missing, so was the neighbor's roof next to Grandma and Grandpa's house. Two young boys were caught out in the storm. Luckily, after being beaten by the large hail, both survived. Part of the high school gym roof was missing.

Tornados can do some pretty strange things. One of Grandma and Grandpa's chairs from their deck was missing. The rest of the set was there, untouched. We never did find that chair. The outer wall of an old civil war era fort once used for protection from hostile forces was also damaged. Every other post from the fence of the fort was lying on the ground. We were all very lucky that no one was killed. I will never forget the sounds and damage this storm caused.

The tornado was not my only encounter with Mother Nature. I fear and respect her. On a similar day, just before the construction of a new garage to our farmhouse, I was standing on the concrete steps outside our home. I was about nine years old and was watching a storm develop in the western sky. Lightning began so I moved closer to the screen door that led into our utility room.

The main storm seemed to be about ten or so miles away, but what I quickly learned, lightning both precedes and follows storms. I felt the particles in the air electrify. It felt like static as the hair on my arms and head came alive. A bright flash struck the end of our driveway. A visible ray shot past me on the ground about three feet from where I was standing. My mother grabbed me and pulled me through the screen door. An immediate explosion of thunder deafened everything around me. I was paralyzed and had never experienced anything like this before. To this day, I am pretty good at predicting storms, but I do it from the safety of my living room.

Loss

Oftentimes as a child, one of life's inevitable lessons is loss. It may start with a family pet, or maybe something as simple as a foot race. For me, my experience of loss started with a classmate of mine. I was ten years old and didn't understand why my friend couldn't do the things he used to do. Cancer seemed pretty foreign to me, especially as it was associated with a child. We used to play together when I stayed at Grandpa and Grandma's house. He liked magic tricks and playing jokes. One day he was just not able to come to class. It had been some time since we had seen him in school. In the middle of the day, one of my other classmate's Father, a local minister, came to our classroom. He tearfully announced that our classmate, my friend, had died. It felt like this was all a dream. As a parent now, I could not imagine the pain my friend's parents went through.

The next lesson of loss happened shortly after the first. It involved my Grandpa John and Grandma Adeline, my father's parents. Grandpa John was a short, stern man with a quick temper. Grandma Adeline was a hot mess. She loved shoes, clothes, and living a soap opera dream. I learned a great deal of my colorful language by watching the interaction between this pair.

Most of my colorful language was learned by watching Grandpa John scold salesmen who would show up unannounced on our farm. He gave his opinion without filter, often times to Grandma Adeline. Looking back, they could not have been more opposite of each other. As a young boy, I took a trip with them to North Carolina for my grandfather's Army reunion. I rode in the back of their car and really got to know both Grandpa John and Grandma Adeline. I saw Washington, D.C.; Hershey, PA, and a battlefield in Vicksburg, PA. Grandpa was a spirited World War II veteran, tough and hard-headed. He seemed to never have any peace.

One thing about Grandpa John was that he was predictable. Whether it be his anger or opinion, you could feel the electricity in the air as the tension would build. The craziest thing he and Grandma Adeline did was purchase a winter home in Texas. I could not imagine Grandpa John making that type of commitment. For the longest time, he would talk about what a waste property like that was, and now he was part of that community.

When I was a child, Grandpa John entered a different kind of war which at that time was rarely won. Cancer. It transformed my Grandpa John from a stoic, tough-talking soldier, to a smaller version of himself that slept most of the day. He pulled an oxygen tank with him wherever he went, which was never far from home. Toward the end, he spoke less than usual. When he did speak, it was a whisper. His hair had turned from dark, to gray, then left him. Cancer eventually took Grandpa John. It was a dark dream to me, like the one experienced when losing my friend and classmate.

Death and grieving were new to me and in processing them, it felt more like a punch in my gut than an emotion. Between attending the prayer service and the funeral, the process seemed to drag on to the point of torture. I didn't understand why it took so long to bury the dead. About an hour before my Grandpa John's funeral, I stood looking at the open casket. It was Grandpa John, kind of, but it really wasn't. Two Army soldiers stood watch on each end of the casket. One of the local women from a church group asked me if I had ever touched a deceased person before. She grabbed my hand and placed it on Grandpa John's forehead. I wished she had not done that. There was no good that came from that act. To me, this was not Grandpa John, he had moved on. I can only hope that he found some peace.

What followed over the next three years was a tragic series of similar situations. Grandpa John had four brothers. In those three years, three of those four brothers died similar deaths. Each funeral, similar to the next. Each feeling similar to the last. I was growing to expect tragedy to strike. Each time was shocking, and I was getting sick of having to participate in these terrible events.

When my Great Uncle Jim was taking cancer treatment, I was about 11 years old. Jim asked my parents if I would be able to ride with him to his treatments. His farm was approximately three miles south of our farm. He was afraid that he would fall asleep on the way back to his home. The hospital was about 35 miles away from his farm.

Great Uncle Jim would pick me up early in the morning. I would accompany him to the hospital and his treatment. I would look around the waiting room and see these people suffering from a disease that had already taken my friend and Grandpa John. After his treatment, Great Uncle Jim would spend a considerable amount of time in the bathroom.

Uncle Jim drove a silver Cadillac with a sloped back. It was ugly but had every option at that time. I really didn't have much going on at 11 years old, and this was a different kind of adventure. Uncle Jim was a bachelor and fighting cancer pretty much on his own. What transpired during the series of his treatments was a secret Uncle Jim and I shared. The reality about Uncle Jim's treatments is that it decimated him. He was hardly able to move after receiving each treatment. I built a bond with Uncle Jim as he taught me how to drive his silver Cadillac. On the way home, we would have to stop several times, he was so ill.

Great Uncle Jim did his own driving on the way to take the treatments. At eleven years old, I drove him back from the treatments, stopping just short of our farm. Then we would switch spots and he would drop me off. Even though we didn't speak much on these trips, I learned a lot from Uncle Jim.

Grandma Adeline and I had always spent a great deal of time together. Living next door during my early years, I quickly learned that if I wanted something that I probably shouldn't have, I went to her. If I was told "no" at home, I knew a cheerful "yes" would ring from her lips and I would get what I wanted. When my brother had a birthday and got a present, I would surely also get a present from my grandma. As a parent, I can see how this would be completely frustrating and unfair to my parents. As a child, I enjoyed the instant gratification of knowing that sticking out my bottom lip and complaining to Grandma Adeline would get me whatever I desired.

In 1987, we received a terrible call. Another tragedy had befallen our family. Grandma Adeline was killed in a car accident near her winter home in Texas. I was told that a drunk driver had crashed into her vehicle. A large chunk of my life was taken in a short period of time. I resented the losses so much, but accepted that life was cruel and unforgiving. Confusion, anger, sadness, and fear followed me wherever I went following the death of so many loved ones. Organized sports became my outlet. Without them, my life would have turned out quite differently. Submitting to the notion that life was short, I moved forward in my own direction. I knew about loss, I didn't fear it any longer. I simply expected it.

After so many tragedies so close together, I felt as if my family was being punished for something. I became very desensitized by the whole funeral process. For each respective funeral, I would critique the music, flowers, casket, and the food after the internment. It was a cold feeling inside, but I knew the funeral process. I was on a first name basis with the funeral directors.

These experiences transformed me into somewhat of a risk taker. I viewed the world as rather temporary. I learned that life was incredibly short, not necessarily beautiful, and the end could come at any time. Looking back, I took an incredible amount of unnecessary risks in the name of sheer fun or just plain ignorance. It was not that I wanted to get hurt or die. Quite the opposite. I wanted to live and feel the excitement before life took me.

The Finer Things in Life

Watching a parent place their child in a "time out" is something most people see on a regular basis. When I was growing up, punishing a misbehavior was swift and depending on where a person was, very public. It was not uncommon to see a child receiving a spanking in the middle of the mall during Christmas season. I want to be clear, I was not abused. I was

disciplined, which included the occasional spanking. As the
middle child, it was my duty to be the shit of the litter. I feel I
lived up to that reputation. Any discipline I received was truly
warranted. It always ended with a lesson and love, however.

As I was writing this book, I asked my father if I could
tell a classic tale of discipline that involved the two of us. He
reluctantly consented. I wanted to write it before that consent
was revoked. For this creative display of education to take place
in today's society would be nothing short of impossible. Back
then, however, I watched my father and the majority of other
adults his age, indulge in several cigarettes a day. I thought
nothing of it. There was a smoking lounge almost everywhere,
including church. People smoked in their cars, homes, and in
high schools. My pediatrician couldn't finish an exam without a
smoke break. My father's brand was Vantage.

I knew where he kept these mysterious little sticks of
fire. I decided one day that I wanted to try out what everyone
else was doing. I noticed these cigarettes were Vantage Light,
indicating they must be a healthier choice. I took a pack of my
father's cigarettes and sneaked outside. Why I didn't go further,
I have no idea. I walked about 30 feet from the house and hid by
a tree. With lighter in hand, I lit that cigarette and took a puff.
No offense to Vantage brand cigarettes, but it was pretty bad.
What I didn't know was that I was busted. Apparently, the tree
did not conceal the plume of smoke rolling out from behind it. I
was called to the front step to answer for my transgressions.

What would my punishment be? I was about 8 years old at the time, a little old for a spanking. Like a judge in a black robe, my father handed down my sentence. I was to smoke what was left in the pack until they were all gone. Surely this would make me so sick I would never smoke again. I grabbed one and lit up. I asked my father, "So how do the crops look this year?" I think it took him off guard because we proceeded to have a lengthy conversation about planting and harvest. When I reached the last cigarette, my head was buzzing, but I was still on my feet. This was not having the effect that my father was hoping for.

Already committed to this punishment, my father dug out a cigar. He lit it up and handed it to me. I was to finish this as well. Cigars take a long time to smoke. If someone would have had a camera at the time, they would have seen a father, sitting on the steps of the house, watching his son carry out his required punishment while the son was smoking a cigar and riding his bicycle. Needless to say, I think he made his point because he actually stopped smoking after this punishment. As for me, I don't smoke cigarettes, but I do enjoy a fine cigar on occasion.

The Elmer

My grandparents on my mother's side could not have been more different that those on my father's side. My Grandpa's real name was Harry, but he went by Elmer. His hair was white as snow. His sneaky grin was enough to make you wonder what he was thinking. His wife, Grandma Doris was a gem. Their home always smelled of baked apples coated with cinnamon sugar.

Grandpa Elmer and Grandma Doris lived in a small house in a historic town. Next door was a vacant building once used by cowboys and transient soldiers. On the exterior of the building a person could still read the name "Golden West Hotel". It was a large, spooky building that consumed the entire lot on which it rested.

Behind the Golden West Hotel was Grandpa Elmer's garden. Grandpa Elmer's garden was always lush as if he had a personal relationship with each seed. What was most incredible about Grandpa Elmer's garden was that it was located on the ground of the former ancient junk pile of the Golden West Hotel. The beauty of that garden on such an unlikely foundation is testament to the fact that whatever Grandpa Elmer did, he was quietly the best.

I love baseball. My brother and I were playing catch in Grandpa Elmer's back yard one summer day. He was push mowing and saw us tossing the ball back and forth. He shut the mower off and walked up to my brother. "I will show you a couple of pitches that will really get them," he said. My brother handed Grandpa Elmer the ball. How bad could this be? My 75-year-old grandpa was going to throw the ball at me and I was going to catch it like I had done a million times before.

Grandpa Elmer turned his engineers' hat to the side and proceeded to conduct a wind up as if he was a major league closer. He launched the ball in my direction. My eyes began tracking this white orb hurling at my own head, then my arm, then my head again. I closed my eyes and held my glove open to protect my face. The ball smacked the leather as it dug into my glove. It was terrifying.

"Toss it back," he said. I reluctantly tossed the ball back to Grandpa Elmer. "This one I call the old roundhouse!" He proudly exclaimed.

Holy crap! Now he is naming the pitches! I didn't know if what I witnessed was even physically possible. The ball cork screwed at me like a curly fry. I just dove out of the way. Grandpa Elmer was an amazing pitcher!

When Grandpa Elmer and Grandma Doris got older, my brother and I would pulled our mower on a trailer to their house. Every time we mowed their lawn, my brother and I had an argument. We didn't get paid cash for mowing, but instead, Grandpa Elmer took one of us in his car "uptown" to the local grocery story for a soda and a candy bar while the other one continued to mow.

Grandpa Elmer should not have been driving at the time. We would slowly travel down the street and come upon a stop sign for main avenue. Apparently, the stop sign was a mere suggestion for Grandpa Elmer because we would always float right through.   It was a three-block ride of terror.

One day we had safely made it to a parking spot outside the store. Grandpa Elmer parked next to a Sheriff's Department squad car. Considering that no respectable DOT person would pass this vehicle as safe for transportation on a public road, I was a bit concerned. To make matter worse, I was certain that the vehicle tabs expired a good decade prior to our most recent trip. Insurance? I didn't even want to know. Grandpa Elmer looked at the Sheriff and gave him a grin. The Sheriff said, "Afternoon Elmer!" and pulled away.

Grandpa Elmer was the master at whatever he did.

You never knew what Grandpa Elmer knew. He would just surprise you with a talent out of nowhere. One day, he just stood up from a crossword puzzle he was working on, walked up to a piano, started playing, and sang a song.

I wish I would have gotten to know Grandpa Elmer better. All too soon, he passed away after working in his garden. He came in from outside and sat down in his favorite recliner. He turned on his favorite program, "Little House on the Prairie". Grandpa Elmer closed his eyes and went to sleep, never to wake again. He was even able to master dying.

Go Carts and Other Dangerous Things

Whether or not you believe in God, angels, guardians, or the supernatural, I am fairly certain that whoever is protecting me typically has a hand on their forehead in disgust.

I learned to drive at a very young age. One of the best projects that my brother and I shared with our father was the building of a go cart. It was an innovative design and is still in my brother's possession to this day. We rode this go cart all over the farm. Driving down our long driveway as fast as we could, we would lock up the brakes and spin around on the gravel.

One summer, the county had just paved the road at the end of our driveway. I left the yard on the go cart. I had the throttle wide open, headed towards the end of the driveway as I had done many times before. I would get to the end of the driveway and u turn on the new pavement. I was nearing the end

of the driveway when I heard a voice in my left ear, "Hey Dan!"
The voice was my own, loud, and clear.

I looked to the left and coming quickly was a white
touring motorcycle headed westbound. Someone, from
somewhere, warned me of this oncoming motorcycle. If I would
have completed my U-turn, I would have been T-boned by a
large motorcycle. I have a belief in where the voice came from;
others may draw their own conclusions. I can tell you this
though; I was being looked after and was very grateful. I didn't
ride that go cart for some time after that near miss.

Motorcycles have always been a part of my life, even as
a child. I started my motorcycle riding on quite a machine. An
early 1970's model Yamaha Mini-Enduro. This 60cc
powerhouse propelled me screaming forward at top speeds in
excess of 28 mph. Equipped with a headlight and horn, this little
gem taught me many valuable lessons.

Of course, my older brother had to have a bigger and
faster motorcycle. One of our favorite activities was to play
chase. Having a long driveway and a good size farm makes
conditions ideal for a good game of motorcycle chase. Make no
mistake, there were rules set forth by our parents. :Not going
under the guide wires that were attached to telephone poles and
the ground" was one of them.

I found that going under guide wires was a pretty
effective way to escape from my brother's larger, and more

powerful motorcycle. Although I had a smaller motorcycle, I learned that maneuverability in tight spaces often gave me an advantage. He would often chase me in open areas where I was clearly easy prey. Sometimes I would head to the grain bin site where I could lose him in a maze of metal. The grain bin site contained several tall, round, and metal structures that stored grain. In between each bin, there was a walking path. My little Endure fit through perfectly. I had the paths memorized and would zip through the maze and appear on the other side.

One day it was my turn to chase my brother. I did not realize that he had also honed his skill of riding through this maze. He had to ride very slowly through the maze as the handlebars of his larger motorcycle nearly touched each bin as he passed. Not so for me, I had the throttle open. As I gained on him this particular day, he turned around and grinned at me. Through my experience, this meant that he had a plan and I was about to be the recipient of some clever trick.

On the top of the grain bins, there were augers. Ropes hung down to the ground, that when pulled, opened slides for samples of each commodity. As he passed by one of the ropes, he grabbed it and flung it outward. I was coming fast at him and couldn't stop. The rope caught the wind and seemed to wait for me. It caught my right handlebar, stopping my minibike and sending me flying.

This was not my first wreck, and other than a little dent in my pride, I was uninjured. We played for keeps.

As the tables turned I was now the prey. The bottom of our ditch had not yet been mowed. My goal was to get to the tall grass and sit there hiding and waiting. The minibike took off as fast as it could. As I approached the road, I looked behind me only to see my brother rounding a corner. I looked forward and realized I was not where I thought I was. The driveway stood about eight feet above the ditch. A person could easily climb one side and safely roll down the other on our driveway except for one spot. There was a culvert that allowed water to flow under the road from one side of a ditch to another. The ditch had a gradual slope on one side and was straight down on the other. I was already up the sloped side and headed for the straight downside.

The minibike didn't fly like the General Lee on the "Dukes of Hazzard". It simply went across the road and dropped straight down. I landed with a thud and both tires exploded as they impacted the ground. The bike was still running as I sat in head tall weeds with my mouth wide open. If, as a man, you could imagine falling eight feet onto a metal gas tank, groin first, you can probably imagine why my mouth was wide open. After some time to recover, I emerged from the tall grass pushing my minibike. I don't believe I ever rode that little minibike again. I needed something bigger and faster. This incident could easily have been fatal, but at least it didn't happen under a guide wire.

<u>Sno-Jet</u>

Snowmobile, Snow machine, call it what you will. The slang term in the north land is "Sled". Living where there is a large amount of snow, snowmobiles zip up and down snow-covered ground where most vehicles cannot travel. On some occasions, they may be the only mode of transportation available due to large volumes of snow.

The snowmobile is like a motorcycle for winter conditions. It is an engine that powers a rubber track, guided by a series of wheels and rails. The handlebars are connected to a set of skis which steer the snowmobile left or right. Steering is not an exact science. Like a boat, a snowmobile does not immediately turn when the driver moves the handlebars. The machine slides and slowly makes the turn. Drivers must plan their turns well in advance to avoid missing their target.

We had a snowmobile called a Sno-Jet. It was old, took forever to start, but once running, was a blue lightning bolt across the white plains. After sitting all summer, trying to get the Sno-Jet to run was always a daunting task. The sled sat behind our house all summer long. When it was finally winter and time to start the process of getting it to run, it would be an all-day event. After hours of pulling on the starting rope, disassembling the carburetor, drying spark plugs, patience and tempers became very thin. A new accessory on our Sno-Jet one

year, was a crack in the fiberglass hood. If I had taken my
father's boot and placed it in the crack, it would miraculously
have been a perfect match. After some physical abuse and curse
words, the Sno-Jet came to life, despite the crack.

What do kids do when it's 0 degrees Fahrenheit and
there is three feet of snow? In my day we got creative with the
Sno-Jet. Tying a rope to the rear of the sled, we attached our
aluminum saucer sled. There were two holes in the top of the
aluminum disk that the rope snaked through perfectly. I wore
my warmest gear and strapped a crash helmet to my head. My
brother gunned the Sno-Jet and off we went.

It is a strange sensation being pulled 50 miles an hour
over snow. There is not much sound other than the sled gliding
across the snow. The ride was faster than I expected. I could
hear my own whimpers as we entered into an open field. Like a
motorboat pulling an inflatable tube, my brother began a slow
series of turns that became faster and faster. Centrifugal force
tried to tip me over, but I leaned in the opposite direction to
counterbalance nature's effect. Every bump of hard snow felt
like a hammer on my rear. As I crossed a gravel road, sparks
from metal on rock began to fly as if someone were twirling
fireworks on the Fourth of July. We coined this maneuver
"Cracking the Whip". Eventually I succumbed to the force and
ended up flying off the sled. I must have slid for 30 yards until I
came to a stop. It was just the beginning of this exciting new
game.

Riding on the sled behind the Sno-Jet wasn't always terrifying. One day, my brother pulled me around the farm and then started on a trail through some trees. As he passed through the trail, I noticed that the distance between the trees was beginning to drastically narrow. This was concerning because my aluminum death disk was slightly wider than the Sno-Jet. Traveling about 15 miles per hour the Sno-Jet narrowly cleared that last two trees. The rope connecting me to the sled was approximately 25 feet long. Approaching the narrow passage, I put my head down. I felt the impact on both side of the aluminum disk. Bouncing quickly from one side of a tree and ricocheting off the next, I was folded into an aluminum taco. The aluminum disk had folded like a crisp taco shell and I was its contents. A person would think that whoever was driving the snowmobile would quickly stop. Apparently, my brother was laughing too hard to consider that option. Thank goodness the rope snapped or I probably would have continued to be dragged like a spinner bait trying to lure a northern pike to bite a hook.

I am pretty sure you cannot buy these aluminum sleds anymore. I have seen similar sleds, but they're not near the quality. There is probably good reason that local stores do not carry them. If I ever come across one, I will own it. The original taco/spinner sled is at my brother's house and hangs on his wall. The crease is still evident from the taco incident, along with other wounds in its armor from the miles of torture that we both endured. When I sit in that room I stare at that sled and it brings back memories of a less complicated time. I guess in many ways, that old dented sled and I have quite a bit in common.

<u>Independence Day</u>

From what I know, fireworks production is a regulated industry. The power of lady finger firecrackers and Black Cat bottle rockets seems to have changed over the years. I am not an explosives expert, but it just does not seem you get your "bang for your buck" when it comes to the power of fireworks.

There are videos currently online where young people are having a fireworks war with Roman Candles. To the inexperienced eye, one may think that this is absolutely a horrible idea. They may be right. I have a tough time watching these videos because I laugh so hard my eyes fill with tears. I know it is not safe, but it takes me back to our annual fireworks battles.

Every fourth of July I would receive a small stipend to purchase my fireworks. It was good lesson in economics. I had a certain amount of cash and I could buy several little things, or couple of large displays and call it good. I would methodically make my way up and down the firework stands isles, picking out items that I could use to defend my fort. My brother would do the same. We would combine each respective inventories with our neighbors. It would be the older kids against the younger kids, as it always has been.

As the years of these wars progressed, so did the dirty tactics. Because we lived on a farm, there was no shortage of improvised items to employ as weapons. Typically, there were two forts, about 150 feet apart. Endless bottle rockets would be shot back and forth. Smoke bombs would occasionally obscure the land in between the two forts. PVC piping fashioned into gun barrels gave us the best chance of accuracy in case of a full-on frontal assault. The battle would continue until all fireworks had been exhausted. These battles were planned all year. Being captured meant certain torture. Torture could include what we now know as waterboarding or interrogation involving the electric fence, which was meant to keep cattle at bay.

The last battle we would ever have was between my older brother and his friends. My friends and I had taken great pains in fortifying our castle. As in the past, bottle rockets pelted both castles. Occasionally, a bottle rocket would clear a wall and would be met with a screech of pain as it exploded. We had become smart, conserving our supplies. It was clear that our opponents were running low on inventory. We decided to unload on them. With the fury of hell, we pummeled their castle.

During a short break in the action, something hit against the front wall of our castle. It didn't explode, nor did a make a whishing noise as it approached. My friend made a fateful decision. He decided he would investigate this mysterious sound. As he rose, it happened. With a loud splattering sound, his pale skin turned brown. Our enemies had resorted to the use of biological weapons. More specifically, they had shovels and were throwing cow manure at us. We had nothing left to respond. Our supplies were depleted from the last assault.

I needed to respond to this horrendous act. I grabbed a board and angled it in the direction of our foes. They were standing confidently with their shovels in hand. I took one of our last firecrackers and placed it on the board. Looking around the ground, I found a small round rock. I placed the rock on the firecracker and lit the fuse. With a small snap, the rock hurled uncontrollably toward to poop-tossing enemies. With a dull thud, the rock impacted the enemy, knocking him to the ground.

I don't know who won that battle. I do know that it was probably good that this would be the final battle. As we were getting older, we graduated to BB guns, but that is a whole different story.

<u>Bathtubs and Such</u>

It could be stated with certainty: where I grew up influenced the lens through which I see the world. Living on a grain farm seven miles from the nearest town, population 103, one must hone their creative skills. There was not satellite TV, internet, or pay-per-view. It is hard to think that I could live without them today. Instead, I took to drawing, writing, re-arranging my room, and building with Legos. Sports were also great releases and I looked forward to being tortured by two- a-day practices.

You may not think this is possible, but my high school class consisted of about 14 people. I use the word "about" because students would come and go on a regular basis. In a school this size, where often there were under a hundred students, teachers, and other staff, everyone develops much closer relationships than is possible at a bigger school. Just by the small size, it is easy for students to learn personal details of their teachers' lives. It was a laid-back type of education. There was a relationship of trust between parents, teachers, and students. The parents trusted the teacher to educate. The teachers trusted the parents provide their children with values of respect, discipline and hard work. The students trusted if they screwed up, the teachers and the parents would be a united front. Recently, I did a brief volunteer substitute teaching gig. It is clearly not that way anymore. We have lost those valuable relationships somewhere.

A vast majority of the students in my high school came from farms within four small communities. Next to study hall, shop was the premier class to take as a senior. I can say with confidence that I do not believe I ever fixed, built, drew, or created anything of value in shop class. What was created were hours of laughter, fun, mixed with quite a bit of danger. I was not very good with the engines, mediocre at wood working and welding, but for the most part, excelled at independent living.

The high school was situated in the center of town. The football field was immediately to the west and ran parallel to the railroad tracks. The railroad tracks led to the grain elevator. The elevator was a busy place. Throughout the day, grain trucks would be dumping their commodities, leaving only to return to dump more. The post office and fire hall were across the street. The small café and swimming pool were on the east side of town. For a small town, it was a hub of activity.

Small Engine class had very little supervision, which is what made it absolutely awesome. Walking into the shop one day I saw the holy grail. I don't know who owned this death machine, but what sat before me was a cast iron bathtub painted yellow. This was no ordinary bathtub, it was the fastest tub around. Attached to the tub was a framework, set of wheels, foot controls, and handlebars. A makeshift seat sat in the center of the tub. This was the best thing I had ever seen. The owner had affixed a Suzuki 750 cc motorcycle engine to the rear. "That seems a bit excessive" I thought. For fuel, a small beer keg fed the Suzuki motor. The students had been working on this project for some time. What good is a project without a test drive?

I don't know if students these days would get away with the types of risks we took in the name of shop class. I would like to think that when I took the bathtub for a test drive, I was being safe. I mean, I took the time to run to my locker to get my football helmet. Like NASA gearing up for a space shuttle launch, I mounted the tub. The shop door slowly opened, revealing this creation to the world. A group of students rolled the tub, containing me and my life, to the launch pad. The road outside the high school was paved, straight, and flat. This was happening. My flight plan was to keep on the road and not die.

The engine fired up. The tub shook with anger. It was louder than I expected. Because this was a motorcycle engine and transmission, I had to shift it with my feet. There was a nut lying at my feet in the bathtub. I couldn't help but wonder where that little thing belonged. It was too late to worry about that little detail. I shifted to first gear and released the clutch and "The Bath" began to slowly move forward. I steered onto the street and in a short time, turned onto a county road a short distance out of town. The engine hummed as I headed east towards the interstate.

I was in about fourth gear when I met my first vehicle. The vehicle nearly crashed at the sight of my moving bathtub. I had no speedometer, but estimated I was traveling about 45 miles per hour. I had a couple more gears to go should I need them.

I heard a clank as I barreled down the road. It was that nut rolling around in the bottom of the tub. No time to worry about that now.

I nearly reached the overpass by the interstate when I decided to turn around. I had traveled about two miles. Afraid that someone was going to have an accident staring at this guy wearing a football helmet and driving a motorized bathtub, it was time to head back. A grain truck went by and didn't seem to notice me sitting on the approach. I pulled in behind the truck and began my brief journey back to home base.

The grain truck was driving slowly. I could see that there was no one coming in the opposite lane of traffic. "I wonder if anyone has ever passed a grain truck in a bathtub before?", I pondered. I shifted to fifth gear, then sixth. Pulling into the passing lane, the engine screamed as I drove past the grain truck.

The bumps in the road vanished, and everything became smoother. I was in the power band and wondered if maybe I had crashed and was on a divine journey towards heaven. I hoped not as I didn't know what Saint Peter would say about me showing up at the gates of heaven in a motorized, yellow bathtub. (For those that know me, it may not seem too farfetched.) Looking to my right, I saw the grain truck driver looking down at me, looking away, and then looking again. His eyes were wide with amazement, and maybe some confusion. It was one of those looks that a mother gives a child just after they decide to paint the wall with her favorite lipstick.

The bathtub flew passed the grain truck, and I didn't bother using the required hand signals to indicate my next lane change. I steered the bathtub towards the landing pad next to the high school. I don't know how fast I was traveling, but it was enough to make me question my sanity a little.

It can be said that slowing down in life will make you live longer. I cannot disagree. It can also be said that brakes are an essential item on any vehicle be it a car, bicycle, or motorized cast iron bathtub. The bathtub had brakes, kind of. I came in hot, too hot. The smell of burning something and the winding down of the powerful engine filled my nostrils and ears. I down shifted to a stop, just short of the concrete building. The sweat was running down my face under the football helmet. It was a rush, and I was addicted. I would learn later in life that these situations are call "unnecessary risks". If a person survives them, though, they are what make great stories.

As the bell rang and the period ended, there was a sense of accomplishment. When I got home, my mother asked if there was anything new in my life. I did not tell her that I had traveled the speed limit in a makeshift motorized bathtub. I did not die doing this and the act surely would go down in school history. I also passed a grain truck in the bathtub, likely causing the driver to question what he saw and if he should be driving at all. I just said, "not so much."

As for the nut, rolling aimlessly on the floor of the bathtub vehicle, its only function was to hold the steering column in place. Someone needed to fire the person responsible for the preflight check for that potential mishap.

I did share this story with my parents sometime later, safely out of the parental statute of limitations for punishment purposes. Some may ask where the shop teacher was at the time. After he helped push the bathtub to the launch pad, he was out for a smoke. That is small town U.S.A., and I don't know if it exists anymore.

Idle Hands

How does that saying go? "Idle hands are the devil's workshop". Well, I wouldn't say some of the shenanigans we pulled were directed from the devil. I would attribute it more to creativity and boredom. We didn't have movie theaters or arcades within forty miles. We had to entertain ourselves. Unfortunately, some of that entertainment came with risks.

When I was eighteen years old, I didn't really think much about risk. I thought about how to fight the sheer boredom associated with living in a remote part of the country. Helping out on the family farm is a daily responsibility. Heavy rains are something that will bring farming operations to a temporary halt. When things were at a halt, I searched for things to do.

It had rained for about three days straight. The ditches that surrounded the gravel roads were full of water. Short on funds, but rich in creativity, I called up a couple of my friends to see what they had planned for the evening.

David was, and still is, a lifelong friend. He has his own house which seemed to be the local hangout for many of the other farm kids, especially in the evening hours. This warm summer evening it was just David, Jim, and me. Dave didn't have cable, there was no internet, but he did have a truck. After some regular banter, we made the decision to create our own type of fun. Like a quick vote in an executive boardroom, we all decided to try something we were sure no one else had ever done before.

The sun was just descending below the horizon. The rain had stopped, and the ground was like a wet sponge. Dave was a talented water skier. Jim was a talented driver of many vehicles. Me, I was just along for the ride. Grabbing a waterski and some rope, we piled into Dave's Chevy truck and tore out of his yard.

We didn't drive far when we found the perfect spot. A ditch, full of fresh water, that stretched for at least a mile. Dave hopped out and waded into the waste deep water. I grabbed the rope and hooked it to the ball hitch of the Chevy truck. Dave's head was sticking out the water like a turtle checking out its surroundings. I hopped into the bed of the truck facing Dave. With Jim in the driver's seat, I told him to "hit it".

Like the true water skier that he was, Dave popped right out of the water. We were off, making history, one mile of water filled ditch at a time. Jim was driving about 15 miles per hour when we saw another vehicle headed our way. When the driver of the vehicle met us on the narrow gravel road, they nearly hit the opposite ditch. The sight of a Chevy truck pulling a water skier in ditch full of water was surely a sight to behold.

We made a couple more passes that evening, not realizing what could happen if Dave's ski would have caught some debris, or a metal culvert. Proud of our accomplishment we headed back to Dave's house. We all thought that no one in the world would have ever tried such a stunt. Years later, with the popularity of video cameras and the internet, we realized that special night wasn't so special at all. Apparently, there were other people in the world that were as bored as we were.

The Lake

Most people have that one place were some of your best memories become engraved in your mind. Mine was the lake. This wasn't just any lake, this was the best and worst idea ever. Dave's parents owned a lake home on a large Minnesota lake. We went there nearly every available weekend. Dave's parents did not go there. We were responsible kids, but we also loved to push the limit with our fun. What better place to push the limit than a lake home of which we had free reign?

The lake house was the meeting place for parties, small groups of friends, and no adult supervision. We had access to personal watercraft, boats, and other toys that others may not even dream of letting their teenagers touch. Our weekends consisted of mini tacos, onion rings, water skiing, and general horse play. Was there beer? It's the lake, there is always beer.

It was a hot Saturday evening in July that one of the funniest things I had ever seen took place. A small gathering had quickly turned into about 25 people of various ages having a great time at the lake house. Jim and I were low key guys. We kind of just kept to ourselves and enjoyed people watching. One of the guys at the lake house that night had been trying desperately to impress one of the girls. His name was Derek and he was known for his suave approach to girls. Derek had been telling her all of the right things that night. Those words, combined with some liquid encouragement, appeared to be having his desired effect on the young lady.

Jim and I situated our law chairs in the front of the lake house. This was our favorite time of day. The sun would set over the water and the lake would reflect the colors like a mirror. Because it was near July 4, distant fireworks reflected off the water in as they cleared the tree tops, exploding into various colors. The sun set quickly, and darkness fell upon the water.

Jim and I were on our second pack of cigarettes. We had found a stash of fireworks and would randomly shoot one off in the name of freedom. As it became darker, the group inside became louder. I liked sitting outside because I did not like crowds. That is when I noticed a couple of people leaving the lake house.

Derek had long blond hair. Even in the darkness, I could see it was him. With him was the young lady that he had been hunting all evening. It appeared that Derek had worn her down and she had succumbed to his loving words. Jim and I watched as he removed his shirt as they walked to the end of the boat dock. I had a good idea what was about to transpire in the boat we used for waterskiing. I was not going to be the one to clean up that mess. Jim apparently was thinking the same thing.

After watching the two silhouettes at the end the dock, the young lady hopped into the boat. Derek was struggling to get a knot in is swim short drawstring undone. After a short struggle, Derek's shorts were off. In case you didn't know, light colors reflect light. The funny thing about the human body, especially in the summer, is that what the sun doesn't touch, stays extremely white on a Caucasian. Before Jim and I stood a full moon, but not the moon we all enjoy on a hot July evening. This was Derek's moon and it looked like two soft white lightbulbs glowing in the darkness. To Jim, it was the perfect target.

Jim doesn't say much usually, and tonight was no exception. He just let out a little giggle and produced a bottle rocket from the fireworks stash. He slowly held it up to his cigarette and lit the fuse. The sparks danced like a welder placing a hot bead on a fresh piece of steel. Jim leaned back in his lawn chair, pointed the bottle rocket in the direction of Derek's white ass and waited.

With a loud *swoosh,* the bottle rocket was on its way to the intended target. It reminded me of the patriot missiles we saw on television during the first Gulf War. Now bottle rockets are notoriously inaccurate. I don't know where this bottle rocket came from, but it must have had smart technology. As the sparks streamed towards Derek, it looked like a tracer round from an M60 machine gun.

The bottle rocket flew straight and true and the moment it contacted Derek's flesh, it exploded. Sounds tend to carry over water. On a quiet night, you can make out conversations from clear across the lake. I can say with reasonable certainty that Derek's screams were heard in the next county, maybe even the real moon. "Bulls eye!" Jim exclaimed. I couldn't believe what I had just witnessed. Jim calmly sat there like he knew exactly what was going to happen from the second he lit the fuse. I was laughing so hard I was hyperventilating. The young lady jumped out of the boat and ran back up to the lake house. Derek was still down on the dock. Jim and I were still laughing. Poor Derek, he thought he was going to make his mark on yet another young lady. Unfortunately for him, all he received was a painful burn on his left butt cheek. I don't know if Derek ever figured out it was Jim that shot him with the bottle rocket, but it was truly was of the funniest things I had ever seen happen. I loved the lake and never wanted these days to end, but they did.

On the Move

I got up early that day. It was cold, and the ground was white with snow. With two years of college under my belt I had unknowingly set the wheels in motion that would define a great deal of my life. Today was the day I left for basic training. Considering I spent the prior evening cross-country skiing in foot deep snow, some warm San Antonio, Texas weather sounded nice.

I won't go into detail about basic military training. For me, it was rather uneventful. Like Forrest Gump, it was easy for me to simply do what I was told. What can be said is that basic training, regardless of the branch, is a complete culture shock. If it was a new concept, it would probably be promoted as a new hit reality television show. People from all over the United States are put into a room to live together for many weeks. These people have different values, beliefs, and quite a bit different views on work ethics. There were people who had accents I could not even understand. And there were fights, big and physical fights. I think it is part of the whole process, because like a well-oiled machine, everyone seemed to be on the same team and page when we graduated.

After basic training, I came back to start my life. The plan was to find a job and finish my last two years of college. I wanted that bachelor's degree. The military offered the benefits and tools that I needed to achieve that goal. I found a quiet one room efficiency in the north part of the city. You could call it two rooms if you count the bathroom. I had a hot plate for a kitchen, a small fridge, and a day bed. It was perfect.

I loved guard drills. I was a Combat Arms Training and Maintenance Instructor (CATM). We were assigned to the Security Forces Flight and wore bright red baseball caps that read "Combat Arms" in bold black letters. I felt a sense of family with my guard unit. I loved my job as an armorer and instructor. Hours of practice gave me confidence in my marksmanship and

instructional abilities. Receiving a small paycheck was also a
great perk. The 1984 Pontiac Grand Prix that I drove in high
school still ticked along, so I had no vehicle payment. The small
commission check from my job in treadmill and exercise
equipment sales paid for food and rent. This wouldn't make me
rich, but I was maintaining, and more importantly, stable.

Guns and Stuff

Just because a person is good at something, doesn't
necessarily mean they are in love with it. There are people that
are awesome at listening to others, for example, and then can
offer guidance and advice. Some of those people can not stand
listening to another person's problems, but they do it because it
helps others and they happen to be good at it. My talent seemed
to be marksmanship. It was a challenge, and a perishable skill.
Years of shooting as a child, almost daily, honed my
marksmanship skills. Shooting, like many sports always gave an
opportunity for improvement. My dad still tells the story of how
upset my mother would get because I would shoot the clothes
pins off the wire of her clothes line.

Considering my rural upbringing, guns were more a part
of life than just a topic at a party or gathering. Everyone had
them, everyone used them for either hunting or home defense.

The thought of someone taking a gun and using it to enter a building or school to inflict harm upon others was not even conceivable.

It may come as a surprise to those who know me, but for all the years of shooting and training, guns were mere tools and really provided me no interest. Shooting is like knowledge. I thought of it as a honed skill that could keep me alive and protect others. Other than that, I don't dream about shooting perfect scores or owning the latest gun. I can hold my own with the best of them at a shooting competition but if I never participated in that activity, it would be fine. Make no mistake, I have several guns, and one is with me nearly everywhere I go. More importantly, I know how to use it. Fortunately my career allows me to arm myself. Anything can happen, it's a big bad world out there.

Deputy Dan

An opportunity arose out of the blue, or in this case, brown. In the newspaper classified section, the Sheriff's office was looking for applicants to be part-time reserve deputies. Essentially, the Sheriff's office would provide all the necessary training to become a part-time peace officer for their department. Candidates would work in the jail, with a deputy, but were needed primarily for special events. It was truly my first taste of authority versus the public. In a small community such as this, often times authority involves the enforcement of laws against people you have known your entire life. I was okay with that challenge.

I applied, interviewed, and didn't come anywhere close to getting the position. After about four or five months, the advertisement came out again. This time I was more prepared and was selected. The class I started with are now primarily full-time officers, deputies, and federal agents. And there is surely one from that group who will become sheriff of that county where I was given my first taste of civilian law enforcement. But at that time, all I knew was that Deputy Dan had a part-time peace officer license and was ready to take on the world.

USA

Growing up watching the Olympics was always fascinating, so when my first true deployment came up, it seemed more of a once-in-a-lifetime opportunity than work. It was the summer of 1996 and the Olympics were held in Atlanta, GA. My unit was given the opportunity to be part of the supplemental security force in support of Olympic operations. After two years as a deputy, I had not even left the state. Being part of the security at the Olympics was an opportunity to not only see but be part of history.

My unit hummed down to Atlanta on a C130 military transport plane. We were herded through long lines and given credentials. The anticipation of what venue we would be supporting made my heart race. We were transported to our barracks on a bus. The barracks weren't barracks at all. The barracks was an old airline training facility full of bunk beds. Inside the building was a massive open room the size of a closed Kmart. It was dark because people were working different shifts. The air was stale and smelled of foot powder, Ben Gay, and mold. This would be our home for the deployment. It didn't matter, it was the Olympics.

The day came when we were told what venue we would be supporting. I was in full anticipation mode. "Would it be track and field? Or maybe basketball! This was the year of the "Dream Team"! Please let it be basketball!"

Not even close. The expression on my face was probably like the first runner up in the Miss USA competition: Not so happy. "Women's Field Hockey" was my assignment. Thinking apparently out loud, I said, "I don't even know what the hell that is." No offense to field hockey athletes around the world, but being from North Dakota, it just isn't on the list of extracurricular activities. In North Dakota, hockey is typically associated with stinky gloves, emotional fans, and ice. Field hockey or not, this was going to be an experience and I was excited to be there. Maybe this field hockey thing would be completely awesome.

Field hockey for me was not awesome. All the running and the strange rules. I looked forward to people watching and potential days off. This was a new world that needed exploring. There was a magic in the air simply because it was the Olympics. My job was mostly smiling and being friendly to people passing my post. Reality was setting in and as far as my role in Olympic security was concerned, I was as important as a traffic cone.

Finally, a day off came to explore Atlanta. Another guy from my unit and I took off to see what type of shenanigans were afoot in this magic place. We found a jazz sax musician promoting his CD, a street performer showing off magic skills, and a local guy who wanted to show us a shortcut to Olympic village. What a nice guy. Something didn't seem right about this local, though.

After about a mile of walking, this nice guy told us that around the next corner was his "crew" and we had best pay him, so his crew didn't have to collect. My suspicions were confirmed. This was no nice guy. I grabbed the local and told him, "Listen douche, I will ruin everyone's day right now if you don't run." I had been working on my communication skills and in this instant, it paid off. The local quickly submitted and scurried off down the street in search of his next potential victim. We walked on, minus the local, towards Olympic village.

Obviously unfamiliar with the area, we headed towards the sound of music, crowds and what we knew was Olympic village. We were about two to three blocks away, when all hell broke loose. Pop! Thud! Sounds, not like a shotgun, bigger, more aggressive, ripped through the noise of the bustling crowd. What was happening? The music didn't stop right away, but kind of died off, one instrument by one instrument. People began rushing in all directions. Chaos. We needed to get somewhere other than here. There was something not right.

We quickly learned that the sharp noise we heard was some sort of explosion in Olympic park. We heard that people had been injured. We needed to contact other members of our guard unit. We fought our way back to the train terminal. It was going to be a longer than normal ride back to the barracks. Because of the chaos that ensued after the explosion, several thousand people were on the move. It took nearly two hours to get back to our barracks. We were the last to report in to our Lieutenant. Thankfully, all our members were accounted for and safe.

To date myself just a little, I stood in line for the local payphone, calling card in hand. We were instructed to phone our relatives and inform them that we were safe yet provide no further information. I don't believe anyone had a cell phone nor were they very prevalent at the time. Regardless, I could not have afforded a cell phone if I had wanted one.

I tried several times that day, to call home using my calling card. However, all circuits were busy. After numerous attempts, I was able to contact a friend and have them pass information regarding my safety on to my family. I laid down on my bunk after the call and stared at the stained tile ceiling. Today I was almost robbed and witnessed a violent act that would become part of American history. I volunteered to work every day until the end of deployment because here in Atlanta, days off were absolutely exhausting. I put on my headphones and fell asleep to my Meat Puppets CD.

An Uncertain Future

There is always a point in life where your future is anything but certain. In college, taking expensive classes that meant very little, the direction of my life had seemed to have taken some sort of hiatus. I had my guard drills, my work, volunteer deputy gig, and school. There were no potential career leads and my impending graduation from college was just around the corner.

I had decided that I was built for the law enforcement machine. It was who I was. Law enforcement positions in this area were not easy to come by. I would need to make myself marketable. I didn't realize it at the time, but I had already started this process. My choice to finish my college studies, volunteer, and work would eventually pay off.

After two years of collegiate boredom and selling treadmills at a local retailer, the light at the end of this tunnel was shining bright. Taking one or two summer classes helped shorten my educational path and I was now only three credits short, so it appeared I had only one class left. Upon speaking to my advisor, I was told that I never received my physical education credits from basic training. The ROTC staff signed off on those credits. Just like that, in a matter of two hours, I had unexpectedly graduated from college. This was not part of the plan, but it was welcomed.

In May 1996, I graduated with my bachelor's degree in Sociology from North Dakota State University, Go Bison. I was not a fan of school. A little restless to start my life, I didn't care to reminisce about the good old days. I preferred to look forward and tackle what was next. There were still two years of eligibility left on my GI Bill, but I had already achieved my goal. I had to find a new tunnel.

<u>**You Have to Try**</u>

If you want to get hired, you must try. That means filling out endless applications and submitting them via the U.S. Postal Service. Please remember, this is a time where word processing programs and email were inconceivable things of the future. Slowly and methodically, I typed application after application to various law enforcement agencies. I knew that some of the smaller agencies budgets were probably tight. That meant that a good candidate that had already been to the initial training, would be a marketable item on a resume.

The two most prolific applications arrived in the mail. The North Dakota State Highway Patrol and the Fargo Police Department. I had my eyes set on the North Dakota Highway Patrol. The idea of my own squad, out there on the road, wearing that big round hat was almost too irresistible. Experience told me that a hand-written application typically would go to the bottom of either a pile or waste basket. Turning on the electric typewriter, the warm air blew out in sync with the cooling fan. With the snap of each key, letter by letter was imprinted on the application. It took two separate afternoons slowly typing these applications. Once completed, they were mailed to their respective destinations. Now, the waiting game again.

I received a letter from the North Dakota Highway Patrol indicating that I had been selected for further testing and an interview. Early in the morning, my dad packed me up into our diesel suburban and we started our adventure out to Bismarck, the state capital. It was a sloppy time of year where passing vehicles sprayed slush and salt on our windows. The windshield washer pump was not working correctly, so dad carried several one-gallon jugs of water to rinse off the windshield when we could no longer safely see the road.

The testing was straight forward and I thought I did well. Notifications of who was to continue in the process would be sent out later. The excitement was building inside me. I had accepted that if I was going to get into law enforcement, it would be as a North Dakota State Trooper.

Basic Training Again

The military afforded me several opportunities. One of the benefits at the time was a collegiate tuition waiver. The second was the GI Bill, a monthly tax-free subsidy. About two months after I submitted my applications for various departments, I applied for and was accepted into a privately-run peace officer training program. This program provided all the necessary requirements to become eligible to be a full-time police officer. If I graduated and was hired by a department, I would need no further required training other than what a department would mandate. Luckily, this was a college and my tuition waiver applied. I had no apartment, just my dorm room. I was essentially homeless if I left the campus on the weekends. There was no way I was telling anyone this, I was doing it on my own. My GI Bill was my income and without it, I would have had to figured out how to even fill my gas tank.

Basic peace officer training was something that seemed to fit me like a glove. We had a cast of characters from all over the state. There was a Native American from one of the reservations. A husband, wife, and brother from a small town in the southeast part of the state. There were two mothers that decided that law enforcement was something that they wanted to pursue. There were loud people, quiet people, and those who were right down the middle. This was going to be good time.

From day one I hit it off with PJ. To this day, PJ and I speak on a regular basis. PJ was a big dude. Growing up on or near one of the local reservations, PJ had seen and lived some awesome experiences. Incredibly positive, witty, and willing to play a joke on the best of people, PJ and I would pull shenanigans on everyone, including each other.

The training in this program seemed to come as if it had always been part of me. The list of instructors included the course facilitator, a guy that owned a meat market and his assistant, a personal trainer, defense attorney, and several guest instructors. The Program Coordinator was super motivated. He was approachable and lived his entire life on the thin blue line, a cop's cop.

The physical training block was typically scheduled for early morning hours. The personal trainer, a mid-forties woman who clearly had zero percent body fat, was the epitome of a morning person. It was always the same routine. "Today we are going to start with the mile" she proclaimed. I hated the mile warm up. PJ was always able to imitate her perfectly. After our mile warm up, the true torture began. We were introduced to planks, steps, isometrics, and sprints. It was hard to hate the hard body instructor. Some mornings she put us through hell, but she was the kind of person you didn't want to disappoint.

At the time of my initial training, defensive tactics were the control techniques that were taught to law enforcement officers to safely take subjects into custody and encourage compliance from uncooperative individuals. It included grips, holds, and pressure points. This training was taught by a small local man who had some type of ninja degree black belt. He was terrifyingly calm, spoke quietly, and as demonstrated on his poor assistant, was able to kick someone's ass at the drop of a hat.

At a demonstration during one of our blocks of instructions, his assistant was to attack him. It was like watching an episode of Kung Fu. The assistant approached the instructor from multiple angles. Each time, the assistant ended up flying through the air and on the ground. The last attempt was the worst for the assistant. Coming in at 100 percent, the assistant grabbed the instructor's uniform. In the blink of an eye, the instructor was behind the assistant, and had some crazy hold that incorporated the assistant's own shirt. In a matter of seconds, it was lights out. The assistant laid motionless on the mat. The instructor picked up his victim's feet and slapped them hard. Slowly the assistant's eyes opened, and he sat in an upright position. I had never seen anything like it, nor do I know the customs and courtesies of a dojo. I began to clap, which caused the others to clap. Another lesson that I may never use, don't clap for a dojo.

Scenarios

Scenario- based training is a double-edged sword. It affords students the opportunity to practice skills and make mistakes in a safe environment. If the scenario is good, it is winnable. Also, if the scenario is good, it can also be failed. This balance has created both positive and negative feedback experiences. An overzealous instructor can create a scenario that is so far fetched that it will frustrate a student, and nothing is learned. This is unfortunately the case at several training academies. A good scenario can be simple, maybe with a twist that simply challenges the student, but also can still be completed successfully. Scenarios are part of almost every training I have attended related to law enforcement.

As our training progressed, we were measured on our retention of handcuffing, defensive tactics, the law, and verbal confrontation by having to complete a variety of scenarios. PJ and I teamed up and entered the hallway while one of our scenarios was being arranged. We were told that a fellow student and an instructor would be the role players for the scenario. The story was that we were a double car (two officers on patrol together) being called to a bar where a female subject was intoxicated and refusing to leave. This seemed to be a straight forward situation, but if it was a real call, there would be a variety of inherent dangers we would have to take into consideration.

To describe PJ and me at the time would be rather comical. We both had some size to us. I was into weight lifting and PJ was just a big dude. Together, I am sure we looked as if we could have been a contending World Wrestling Federation tag team. As our scenario began, PJ and I cruised through the door to the scenario. Sitting in the middle of the mat room was a chair and our problem female, one of our fellow classmates. The other instructor was posing as the bartender. The bartender told us that the female had been drinking heavily for several hours and was refusing to leave. The student was really into her role. She began acting drunk, cussing at the bartender and at us.

"Police. Time to go Ma'am. The bar is closing. We will get you home," I said.

She shot a line of profanities at us and refused to move. It was interesting how comfortable this student was in this role. Maybe she was reliving an experience that happened in her life? Without a moment's hesitation, I grabbed her arm and part of her shirt and PJ grabbed her other arm and shirt sleeve. This brought our female subject immediately to her feet. Her mistake was to really get into her role and want to resist. I pulled to the right and PJ pulled to the left. This motion tore this girl's V neck t-shirt from the point of the V front and back. And there she stood, D- sized breasts holstered by her bra, in front of everyone.

It must have been like that dream many people have, the one where you are naked in front of a class. However, she was *really* missing her top now, in front of her class. Without missing a beat, PJ said, "Stop fighting with us or the pants are next!"

"Out of role!" screamed the instructor. We must have passed the scenario as we ultimately were able to move on to the next block of instruction. However, PJ and I were not asked to complete any further scenarios that day.

Domestic Violence

As the blocks of instruction at the academy progressed, so did the intensity of our scenarios. With training weapons by our side, the instructors informed us that we would be responding as two officers to a domestic where the male subject was possibly armed. Guess what? PJ and I got teamed up again to deal with this. As we climbed the stairs, training weapons out, we encountered an individual role player who was not one of our classmates. The role player was an instructor and police officer from the Bismarck Police Department.

We had the subject stand as we went through the proper clearing procedure before we went hands on with him. As we approached, his compliance deteriorated. This time PJ and I were on the same page and moved with sumo- like swiftness. If you ever had to lift a box that you thought was heavy and prepared to lift it, only to realize after throwing it across the room that it was empty, you know what happened next. The suspect left the ground and was propelled into the make shift wall. The wall did not hold the role player. He passed through it as if it were not even there.

The wall was placed there to move the configuration of the room as well as shield the other students from seeing what the scenario entailed. Standing before us were the next students,

anxiously awaiting their scenario. "Jesus you two, out of role!"
screamed the instructor.

For us, the scenarios had ended. The irony of that day
is that the role player that was thrown through the wall still
speaks of it. After my military deployment and a position with a
federal agency, he is now my partner.

Pepper Spray Day

I do not need to be shot to know what it feels like. I do
not need to be hit with a taser to know what it feels like. I also
did not believe I needed to be pepper sprayed to know that it hurt
like hell. In reality, a person should experience two out of the
three to understand how to cope with the effects should it happen
in the course of his job. Learning about the effects of pepper
spray was interesting. As one of the less than lethal tools we
would be potentially carrying, we were required to have pepper
spray blasted in our eyes, then fight through a brief scenario.

Motivated and wanting to get it over with, I volunteered
to go towards the front of the line. The instructor told me that
they would be using a newer, pepper foam, lime green in color.
"Whatever, let's just do this and get it done," I thought to
myself.

Before I got the thought out of my head, the foam impacted my forehead, eyes and nose. Nothing at first, but then the fires of hell started to burn on my very white Norwegian skin. This sucked bad. I completed the handcuffing scenario and immediately went for the water. The cool water soothed the burn, but the second it was taken away, the fire returned with a vengeance. What seemed like an eternity was probably only about 20 minutes of applying cold water, waiting, burning, and applying more cold water. PJ was laughing uncontrollably. All he could see was this lime green blob on my face. It looked like Slimer from Ghostbusters was riding on my head. I could not wait for his turn.

What they tell you and you often soon forget, is that the effects of pepper spray can come back a short time later if moisture is applied to the area where the pepper spray contacted. One by one, each student completed their pepper spray torture. One of the smaller, more timid students really took the spray hard. I figured that is why after the scenarios and pepper spray, we were done for the day. It was off to the showers.

There were a series of about five individual showers with privacy curtains at the training facility. Students would often have to wait their turn. As I was waiting in line I heard grunts and moans of pain from individual showers as people started to relive the effects of the pepper spray as water sprayed on their faces. PJ came barreling out of the shower, as naked as the day he was born. He grabbed a towel and covered his eyes.

"Oh my God! More water!" He turned to go back into his individual shower to try and alleviate some of his pain. With his eyes closed, PJ misjudged the entrance of his shower and headed for the occupied shower that was next to his. Inside this shower was the quiet, timid student who was struggling with his own pepper spray issues. His nightmare was about to get worse.

Could I have said something? I most certainly could have. Would you have said something? In our line of work, I would guess not. Inside that shower was now two naked students, who would soon become very aware of PJ's error. It didn't take long before the complaints of burning eyes turned to the shouting of a terrified student sharing a very intimate space by a larger student who inadvertently entered and started sharing a shower with him. You would think there would be apologies, but it was more confusion. "Get the hell out of here the student yelled!" "What are you doing in my shower?" PJ shot back. I typically have excellent bladder control, but I had to run to a stall because I don't think I have ever laughed that hard in my life.

Offers Coming

Nearly three quarters of the way through academy training now, a group of us decided to test for the Fargo Police Department. I had not heard anything from the North Dakota

Highway Patrol yet, so police testing proceeded. I whizzed through the test not expecting much of anything. There were at least a couple hundred people applying for approximately four positions. I didn't really think much of this process as I was surely going to be a state trooper. Once the test was completed, we all headed back to the academy to focus on completing our training.

Approximately two weeks later, I was notified by the Fargo Police Department and the Highway Patrol that I was in the top five candidates for both departments. I was told I needed to decide which direction I would pursue. Because it was uncertain where troopers are stationed and that I would have to attend their academy, I decided to pursue employment with the Fargo Police Department.

Jokers

Playing practical jokes on one another is just part of what law enforcement officers do. If you are going to play the joke, you best be able to be the recipient in kind. After the shower incident and the ribbing I gave PJ, I knew it was a matter of time before he retaliated. At the time, I shared a dorm room with another student. When you entered the room, there was a closet on the left and right side, as well as a bed and desk. One side of the small room mirrored the other side of the room.

I had something I needed to do after class one day and walked back to our room. When I got there, I noticed that my dorm room door was cracked open. My roommate was notorious for forgetting to lock our door. PJ and his roommate were immediately next door to us. I knew he had just been waiting like a sniper in the grass for the perfect opportunity.

I slowly opened the door with my foot. The lights were off. I could hear giggling like a bunch of teenagers, coming from PJ's room. As I flipped on the lights, I was expecting the room to be empty, on fire, covered in shaving cream, something. When the light revealed the room, it took me about five seconds to realize what had happened. There was no shaving cream, it was not on fire, but instead neat and tidy, but not as we left it earlier in the day. PJ had taken every item, I mean every item, and perfectly switched them from one side to the other. From the clothes in the closets to the trash in the garbage, it was as if someone had taken a picture, and just reversed the image. I guess it could have been worse. My roommate and I just left it as it was for the remainder of our training. Vengeance would be tenfold, swift, and merciless, however.

The night before graduation was going to be a perfect time for retaliation. It had been about two weeks since our room had been switched from one side to the other. Security and vigilance can get lax with time. When security is in a routine and nothing happens, it provides opportunity. The opportunity came for me when PJ left his door open and unattended.

PJ's roommate was gone until later that evening. PJ had desk duty outside the dorm bay. I had at least an hour before I would be detected. I entered their room and slowly loosened any bolt that secured the supporting bars on PJ's bed. Also, PJ had been complaining about my roommate's alarm clock. There was something definitely wrong with it. Because PJ was next door, this alarm would also wake him. I don't know how do describe the sound of this alarm clock. It sounded like a mother cow starting a moo from her gut, letting it pass through her body, and eventually out her mouth. As the moo got closer to her mouth, it also got progressively louder. The alarm was so guttural, it vibrated the clock all over the concrete floor where my roommate had it sitting. It was a horrible sound that woke up at least half of the dorm bay.

I placed this alarm clock under PJ's bed and set it for 4:00 a.m.

I didn't sleep much that night. I kept checking my watch, just waiting. When 3:59 turned to 4:00, the early morning silence was disturbed by what started like a soft hum. Gradually the hum turned into a painful moan, accompanied by a series of bumps and thuds. The alarm had started to do its dance on the concrete floor under PJ's bed. The only sound louder than the alarm was PJ's voice, "What the hell?" "Come on!" "You assholes!" I was laughing so hard it hurt. The alarm had performed perfectly.

Then I heard a series of smashes, and the groan of the alarm abruptly died off. "You guys are dicks", PJ yelled through the wall. I heard him walking around, kicking what was left of the alarm clock towards their door. Suddenly a crash, louder than the first and sounding like a car wreck, was followed by the sound of metal meeting concrete and accompanied by the clang of pieces of bed sliding across a polished floor. "Come on!" As PJ plopped down on his bed, it systematically disassembled, with him in it. It was perfect, and we were up the rest of the night.

The next day was graduation, and I would never again speak to or see half of these people after that day, but I wouldn't forget them.

Part II

The Police Officer

After a series of background checks, physical assessments, and a polygraph, I was offered a position as a police officer with the Fargo Police Department. I could not believe that I was getting paid to do this job! Being a salaried employee with health benefits of my own was all new to me. My tiny one room apartment was upgraded to a two bedroom and my vehicle situation was also about to change. I had never had a credit card, nor had I really taken out any type of loan. My credit was not bad, just non-existent. My parents agreed to co-sign a loan for a vehicle. All the changes were a bit overwhelming, but in a good way.

It was 1997 and we had a ton of snow that winter. I managed to get through all three phases of my field training, despite the epic weather, and entered my one-year probationary period. I wore the uniform proudly and will never forget my first shift as a solo officer. Because of the flood, we did not have enough squad cars available, so I was driving one of our K9 officer's Chevy Blazer. I worked the power shift and because I was now an extra officer on a shift, I was assigned as the city rover. I responded to whatever call dispatch needed handled. I enjoyed the challenge so much, I believed I would never leave this job, ever!

The snow caused a history making flood. After the flood clean up in the late spring of 1997, I had learned that a cop in an apartment could be quite a hassle for a young officer. Everyone in the building knew what you did, and if there was a problem, there was a knock on your door. To get some privacy, I decided it was time to go house shopping. With the help of a local realtor, I found a small house in a very quiet neighborhood. Walking through this house, I found it was bright, warm, and felt like home. An offer for the home was made at about 11:00 a.m. that day.

Home is truly where the heart can be found. I went to my parent's farm and discussed the house and the offer I'd made earlier that day. On the way back into town that evening, I received a call from my realtor. She told me that the offer on the house had been accepted. It was an amazing feeling! So amazing that I pulled over on the side of the road and threw up a little. Not knowing exactly how mortgages and homeownership worked, I recalled every horror story ever told to me about owning a home. Ultimately, it was the best decision of my life up to that time, and I own the house to this day. My life was on track, and I was ready for the ride. Could they really be paying me to do this job? At the end of my shift, I just could not wait to get back to work.

Sharing Sacred Stories

I will say that most cops are all a little hesitant to share certain stories with people outside the thin blue line. I know that as an officer you must be a representative of every social culture. Being a representative requires trust. A cop by nature does not want to violate the trust of their brothers and sisters or those they are sworn to protect. Yes, like anywhere there are bad apples.

My point is that cops sometimes do not know what reaction we are going to get if we start with our war stories. Well, this is a book of war stories from every social culture that emergency services may encounter. Some are good, some are sad, some you may have handled differently that I did. What it comes down to is, like most, we do the best we can with what we have at the time.

Field Training

When a new officer enters the Field Training, they are held to unreasonable standards and unattainable goals. This is by design. Candidates are to learn by doing, whether that leads to success or failure. The goal of the program is to team a new recruit with three experienced officers known as Field Training Officers or FTOs. Three FTOs guide the recruit through three phases of training. The recruit will also work three different shifts. During the last week of field training, the officer is sent back to his or her original officer for a final evaluation.

The standards are very high during field training. At the end of every shift, the FTO evaluates the recruit's performance while working the shift. The key to success in making it through the program is to get to know each FTO, listen, and do as you are told. Also, do not get your FTO hurt.

Should a recruit's shift evaluation consist of an ass chewing for safety, lack of common sense, or missed contraband, they will know they had a bad shift. It is not the end of the world; however, they will need to do exceptionally well the next shift. Should the recruit's evaluation have comments regarding frayed boot laces or less than polished brass, a recruit can take that information as a compliment. The FTO had to look hard to find something the recruit could improve on during that specific shift. I categorize my FTO's into the Down to Earth, The Eccentric, and the Consummate Professional.

If a recruit consistently fails to achieve the goals of the program, they are often dismissed. On very rare occasions, recruits that may or may not have potential can be extended for additional training. It is often joked that these candidates are sometimes later called Sergeant, Lieutenant, or Deputy Chief.

Phase One

The Down to Earth

I am all about respect. To this day, I respect my phase one FTO. I loved this job and I knew he had a lot to teach me. He was a call officer with years of experience that I could quickly begin to emulate. He was an avid dog lover so our shifts often consisted of listening to talk radio and speaking about dogs. I didn't know right away, but he used these things to help teach me about multitasking.

He would often pick an address and say, "Take me there, the quickest, most direct route." This was at a time before GPS. I had torn the map out of a phone book to learn the streets of which I now patrolled. I studied this map every chance I could. While we traveled to each address, he would start talking about dogs, dog shows, or make comments about what was being discussed on the Dr. Laura Schlessinger radio show.

I was so intent on listening to what he had to say, I would often times unknowingly drive past the address I was seeking for the "the quickest, most direct route." When I would realize my mistake, I would look over at him. He would sit straight forward in his seat with a grin on his face, chuckling. I know this was a teaching point, but what he didn't know was that I was also learning about him. I only admit to falling for this tactic, once, maybe two times. The last time, I sat outside the address while he finished his story about dog training. "Why did you stop" he asked. "Because we are here." I responded. Just like that, the "distract the driver with random dog facts" game was over.

It had been cold and I was three weeks in to my phase one training with my FTO, when I felt I had a good handle on his personality. A strange thing occurs when you work with someone day after day. You start to finish their sentences and know what they are going to do before they even do it. Sometimes you even start to kind of look like each other. We both wore our stocking hats with the bottom portion rolled tight. At one call, one of the people we arrested even asked if I was my FTO's son. I believe I was given a high mark for that on my shift evaluation.

Working an early evening shift one night, we received a call of a disturbance in the Taco Bell drive through. When we arrived, there was a car sitting at an angle blocking the rest of the vehicles from entering the drive through. We approached the driver who was yelling inside his car. I could smell the alcohol the second the door flew open.

When the door flew open, the driver started to get out of the vehicle. He continued to exit the vehicle. He was huge. This guy had to play football or something. My FTO let me take the call. I asked the driver what the problem was. He turned and shot me a wide-eyed stare. His mouth was open and his teeth were clenched together like a dog that was sounding a warning growl. I saw my FTO move into the giant driver's blind spot.

"Why don't you just kill me now!" the driver screamed. Like a crocodile shooting out of the water for some prey, my FTO slipped in close with his leg out. I took two steps and gave the driver a shove. The driver stumbled back, tripped over my FTO's outstretched leg, and we both immediately landed on his back. Needless, to say, the driver refused all tests offered for Driving Under the Influence. He was arrested and taken to jail.

Phase Two

<u>The Consummate Professional</u>

After successfully completing Phase One, I moved on to a different FTO, a real cop's cop. The epitome of a police officer of whom I still hold in the highest regard.

On cold North Dakota night, we received first snow of the year. It was still a balmy 38 degrees so the white covering wouldn't last long. Two hours to go and I would be done with Phase Two of the three-phase field training program. I had my celebration plans all in order. I would go home, have some cereal, go to bed, and wait to go back to work.

One major call missing from my training portfolio was an unattended 103. An 'Unattended 103" meant that someone died an unattended death and the police would need to treat it as a crime scene until otherwise notified.

Hearing the call of an unattended 103 miles away from my assigned beat made me think, "Sucks to be you!" My FTO, however, picked up the microphone and "jumped the call". He volunteered us to take that call – away from our assigned beat -- for training purposes. Oh, by the way the individual had not been checked on for a week and a half.

I can deal with a lot. I can deal with life and death. What I struggle with are the natural things that happen with life and death. I am speaking of vomit, defecation, spit, and other odors associated with the expiration of the human body.

When we arrived at the scene, I climbed a set of stairs that appeared to be made for people half my size and with twice my endurance. When I got half way up, I was introduced to death. Not just what death looked like, but also what it smelled like. To this day, I can pick that odor out from miles away.

I reached the top of the stairs and the odor was unbearable. I opened the door and was greeted by my first dead body. A large man, dressed in only his underwear, had fallen face first into a radiant heater. He had been there for a week and a half. His body had evacuated his bowels into his white underwear and his butt was straight in the air. Another FTO and trainee arrived at the scene. More training for everyone. The foul smell was over-powering.

My Sergeant for phase two was a consummate professional and perfectionist. Probably one of the smartest cops regarding case law, but with minimal people skills. The other trainee and I figured out if we covered our noses with our department issued turtle neck shirts, it would help with the smell. My Sergeant told us to get over it (the smell) and do our jobs.

After the investigative steps were completed, I felt I had learned enough. The local funeral home had been standing by to take the man's body. I heard the clanking of a cart coming up the dangerous stairway. Pushing the cart were two men that appeared to be in their late 70s and who were struggling with the cart itself. I knew how this was going to go.

After my eighth or ninth pair of rubber gloves, we managed to get the deceased into the traditional body bag. This guy was three hundred pounds plus of literal dead weight. I'd had enough. I said I would take the bottom of the cart and just kind of guide it while the two old funeral home people would work together, managing the top end.

I expect people to do their jobs. Apparently the "dead body bag zipper-upper and strap to the cart" guy was on vacation that day, because when we were about three steps from the bottom, one of them at the top, let go. The cart pushed me into the wall, sending this 300-pound dead body off the cart. The force unzipped the bag and the body, half in the bag, we ended up in a waltz position against the wall. Like melting snow on a warm windshield, I slowly slid down past my dance partner and helped the two older men take the cart to their waiting vehicle.

Even with the criticism from the Sergeant I had received earlier, I still got the best scores on my FTO report. No tarnished brass, no frayed boot laces, just, "you did good". I went back to my apartment thinking I would do what I did every night after work. I stopped by the grocery store and picked up some food. I hopped in the shower to get the death off of me. I could not get that smell out of my nose, however, no matter how much I scrubbed. I turned on the TV and sat down on the floor with some fried chicken. What a waste that grocery store run had been. I threw it all away, took a second shower, and went to bed.

Traffic enforcement was highly graded in the FTO program. Standing on a road with moving traffic is always dangerous. My Phase Two FTO always kept his composure. I would say that he was one of the more safety conscious officer's I would ever meet. One thing that they really didn't touch on in the academy were the many different types of radars used for measuring speed. I knew what a radar was, just didn't realize there were so many models out there.

Towards the end of phase two, my FTO decided that we should do a little stationary radar on one of the city's busier four lane roads. I took great pains to back the squad into a not so obvious position. I looked at the KR-10 radar gun with some confusion. I had only ever used this unit while doing moving radar. I could not figure out how I was going to get the radar gun off the windshield and point it at oncoming traffic. With a fast jerk, I pulled the radar gun, bracket, and accompanying suction cups off of the front windshield and pointed the whole works out the driver's side window. It must have looked like a bazooka to oncoming traffic.

My FTO lost it. He started laughing hysterically. When I explained to him that I had never used one of these things before, he showed me how, with minimal effort, the radar gun gently glides off the bracket for handheld use. I will say this, when the oncoming traffic saw this large cannon pointed out of the squad car window, they definitely slowed down. I didn't write one speeding citation that morning, but we both had a great laugh.

He was talented, a mentor and friend that any new officer would aspire to be. For that I thank him. He has moved in a different direction now, but his mentoring and helping children as a counselor is exactly where he needs to be.

The Eccentric

Phase three of field training took me into the heart of the North Dakota winter. The snow was deep and the temperature were deadly cold. My field training became something of a unique situation. We could not get through the streets in conventional vehicles. Instead of the Crown Victoria that only had rear wheel drive, we opted for generic ford Bronco's from the city garage. These Broncos were equipped with four-wheel drive but did not have police lights or any other emergency equipment.

My phase three FTO was quite a character. Infatuated with his dog and his sump pump, we would have to drive to his house several times per shift to check on both. "Great, another dog lover," I thought. It was strange trying to do police work in a non-police vehicle. A great deal of the evaluated criteria required traffic stops and other police work. Because of the deadly weather, we were simply there to respond to calls.

My FTO was infatuated with DUI arrests. He told me if I was able to get a DUI arrest in an unmarked city owned Bronco during a blizzard, I would pass phase three with no problem. On the first night, I did just that. From that day forward, he decided that he no longer needed to sit in the front seat of the Bronco.

Drunk drivers were the focus and he was clearly there to only observe.

At some point during his off hours, he had constructed a portable desk. This desk was more like the activity center on a child's stand up walker. It had a pen holder, clip for a magazine, and a make- shift coffee cup holder. When we got into the vehicle he would climb into the back seat and put his FTO activity center over his lap. Phase three training was coming to an end, and thus far I learned how to construct a portable table, with optional coffee holder, for a Ford Bronco.

It's Going to Get Wet

After completing the Field Training Program, all successful graduates enter a one year probationary period. It is one of those things that you initially think about, but then you just settle in and do what you are trained to do.

Because of the huge amount of snowfall, the prior winter, the spring was going to bring great challenges for the City of Fargo. Geographically, I would describe it as the drain of the bathtub, sitting low in the Red River Valley, and water finds the path of least resistance. The fears of a "100 year flood" began to mount as the snow began to melt. Flood was an understatement, it was going to be a disaster for not only Fargo, but many other towns and cities that domicile along the Red River of the North's banks.

The best news I received was that all officers would be working 12 hour shifts, seven days a week until further notice. I really didn't have anything else going on in my life, so this was great! I had worked hard to be where I was at, my only fear was I didn't want to fail. That was all on me, so I dedicated my whole life to becoming the best officer I could possibly be.

Logistically, having all your officers working every single day, poses vehicle issues. Because we had more officers working than vehicles, I was assigned one of our night shift officer's K-9 vehicles. This was even better considering it was a small SUV with K-9 markings front to back. I was assigned number 315, which indicated that I had no specific area and was considered the city rover.

Putting this into perspective, the police department took a brand new probationary officer, made him the city rover, who is driving a high profile K-9 vehicle. I was good with that and rove the city I did. Honestly, I don't think they had a choice. The water in the river was rising and we were incredibly busy. Some officers were even lugging sand bags in their uniforms to help build the massive wall in the war against the water.

As my radio crackled, I received my first call for service as a police officer. It was a dog that someone had found and requested the police take him to the pound. This was not the lights and siren call that I was hoping for, but again, you have to start somewhere. At the time of this call, I didn't actually put all the pieces of the puzzle together.

When I arrived at the home where the dog had been found, the people gave me a long stare. Looking at my K-9 vehicle, I explained to them that I was simply driving it due to lack of vehicles. Satisfied, they produced the dog that they had found. The people told me that he had been fed and watered, even taken a nap.

Taco was his name. I estimated his weight at about 8 pounds. His big eyes looked down as they handed him to me. Taco was a timid, but healthy chihuahua. When we would take a found animal to the pound, the staff there ensured their health and safety. I typically would try to do everything I could to find an animals owner. I am kind of a cynical guy, so I figured Taco had a traumatic day so we were going to have a little fun.

I placed Taco in the passenger seat of my squad and off we went, but we were not going to the pound. Taco would be my partner for a while. Taco and I took off, preparing to fight crime in the city. I received several laughs and stares that day. To see a K-9 vehicle patrolling the streets with a bald cop and an 8 pound chihuahua with his head out the window nearly caused a couple of traffic accidents. Taco obviously was used to riding in a vehicle and was loving his new found authority.

Taco and I made a couple traffic stops that day. We even responded to someone stealing another's sandbags from a berm they created to prevent flood waters. I did enjoy introducing my new partner as Officer Taco. I would be lying if I told you I kind of thought of making him part of my one person family should no one claim him.

As the calls quieted, Taco and I headed to a local park. It was a cold day, but kids that had been cooped up all winter didn't seem to mind. As I pulled in the parking lot, many of the children came running. I enjoyed this part of my job. Handing out stickers, talking with parents, and interacting with the public. Considering our K-9 officers typically worked the night shift, the kids were especially excited at the potential of meeting one of the local police dogs.

Expecting an 80 pound German Shepard to come flying out the vehicle, the kids stood confused at Taco, the 8 pound law enforcement machine. I explained that Officer Taco can get into the smallest of places where larger dogs cannot. Some of the parents where desperately trying to conceal their laughter. As for Taco, he was in his glory. All of the children petting him and caressing him.

In the distance, one of the kids came running. "Taco!" they exclaimed. Obviously, a familiar voice to Taco, he shot towards the little girl. I knew then, Taco's days working the streets as a K-9 officer were coming to an end. The little girl told me that she knew Taco's owner and provided the address.

I brought Taco home soon after, but not until he got a little treat from me. His owner was an older woman. She told me that Taco has been with her for about four years and is like her child. Taco was a gift to her from her husband, had recently passed. She said Taco was pretty much the last link to her husband that she had. Taco appeared to be an important part in her life. Little did she know, he was kind of important to mine as well.

The short time that Taco and I had together taught me firsthand the importance of Community Oriented Policing. Stopping at a park, simply to handing out stickers, Taco was identified and brought home. Everybody won that day.

I would go on to take several other animal calls in my career, but I would never encounter another Taco.

<u>Train Wreck</u>

I had been on patrol for nearly two years at the time of the train wreck. My car was my office. Referred to as "The Batmobile", I am sure every department has one. Officers at my department were often alone in their cars and relied on other single cars for any type of back up. During a period of the day where the two shifts are simultaneously working, there was a shortage of patrol cars. This would require officers to double up so that the other shift had vehicles.

The downtown officers in Fargo had pretty much identified most of the transients that called the streets their home. A vast majority of the transients had some sort of dependency or addiction issues. In the winter months, the bitter cold could prove a fatal adversary for some of the Fargo residents that called the streets their home. As a downtown beat officer, I would often watch the transients closely to ensure their safety.

I was the driver of a double car, patrolling the downtown beat when the officer I was with and I saw a man staggering as he walked on one of the sidewalks. It was a quiet night in general, so we decided to follow this him to make sure he had a safe place to sleep off his ailment. The man stumbled towards the north border of the downtown area. He didn't have the typical dress or gate of an intoxicated transient; he walked purposefully, but with a slight stagger.

Approximately fifteen minutes had passed when the man reached the railroad tracks at 4th Street North, just shy of 7th Avenue North. In the distance, you could hear the familiar horn of a west bound train ready to rumble through the downtown area. I guessed the train was about a quarter mile away at the time. This is where the man stopped. On the tracks. I parked the squad car about 150 feet from the intersection and got out of the vehicle.

I swear a lot. I still do. I don't necessarily think it is a bad thing. I also often ask questions and don't really expect answers. This was one of those times. "What the hell is that guy doing?" I asked myself, apparently out loud. The train's horn blasted again, and I could feel the ground start to shake under my feet. The man was still standing on the tracks, with his back to us, head down. The red lights at the intersection had been activated and the man was slowly surrounded by the cross arms and the flashing of red beacons. We both yelled at him to get off the tracks. The man just stood there.

I looked to my right as the light of the train grew larger and larger. I guessed the train was no more than 75 yards from the intersection at that point. When I turned my attention back to the man, I expected to see him stumbling away from the train tracks. Instead, I witnessed one of the most terrifying sights that still haunts me today. The man had turned and was facing the train, head down, arms out in a crucifix position. At this point, time stopped, or sped up, I don't know which.

I didn't think I ran, but I had. I ran at a man who was clearly trying to end his life by being struck by a train. I don't know if I yelled, and I doubt he would have heard me if I did. I do remember how much the ground shook as I got closer to the man. The air felt like it was coaxing me closer and closer to my destiny. I took one last glance to the right to see if I could make it. I don't recall seeing the light on the train, only to learn later that was because it was so close that its beam was projected well over my location.

I know how to tackle someone. I mean, I played a little football in my day. I tackled him at the waist of which any collegiate football coach would have been proud. We hit the ground hard, so hard my portable radio microphone went flying around like a helicopter propeller. I look back to find the officer that was with me, but saw nothing but tons of fast moving steel barreling west bound.

If you have ever been too close to a train when it goes past you, you know that there is a strange, vacuum- like phenomenon that happens. The air pulls you towards the train as it travels past.   The vacuum of the train pulled at me and the man that I had tackled. To make matters worse, he began to fight with me, screaming he wanted to die, or something like that. I wasn't sure as my hearing was still not functioning like it should.

Where the hell was my partner?

The ground shook and the sound of steel- on-steel was deafening. The smell of diesel and the roar of the train made it impossible for me to even hear whatever words were coming out of my mouth at the time. The sensation of two large hands pulling us closer to this moving hunk of metal increased with every passing car. I managed to get a foothold on what I believe to be a rail road tie or something sturdy. I knew if I could hang on to this guy and keep my footing, the train would eventually pass by.

The details of what happened next are something I only recently started remembering. It was as if someone hit the fast-forward button. I am a solid guy, about 245 pounds. I remember the sensation of someone grabbing the neck portion of my vest and ripping me to my feet. I looked at the person and it was a fireman. I looked around and it was as if I was on a stage, with an audience of police, fire, and EMS.

My hearing started to come back to me. There were sirens and lights everywhere. I was confused. Focusing on one particular squad car that was clearly way out of their jurisdiction, I wondered, "What the hell were they doing here? What was everyone doing here?"

"Are you okay? Hey! Are you okay?" I looked at the fireman and said, "Ya, why?" "Where is my shoulder mic?" I kept asking. This short interaction seems kind of funny now, but I didn't know why people kept asking me if I was okay. I saw other police officers take the man from the railroad tracks into their custody and to the hospital.

The train had passed and I was finally able to locate my shoulder mic. I turned and saw the officer that was with me, standing on the opposite side of the tracks. That officer was and probably still is, one of the most composed people I have ever met. In that moment, the officer looked physically different, upset, concerned, scared, I don't know or exactly remember. I could see the officer was talking on his shoulder mic, but couldn't hear what was said. I couldn't fully hear until sometime later.

Back at the station I recall giving the shift sergeant a debriefing of what I could remember. It was clearly the worst debrief I have every attempted. I felt confused, almost like being awakened from a deep sleep or dream. I just wanted to get back in my car and go back to work, so I did.

The human mind is an amazing thing. It does whatever it takes to protect what feeds it. It will distort and numb sensations, trauma, and memory, simply to function at its optimum. In short, I was numb. Numb to the facts that occurred just an hour or so before.

That decision to hop in a single squad car by myself and finish out my shift changed my life. It was the wrong decision. In the time when I was a proud patrol officer, I am certain that same wrong decision was made countless times at departments all over the world. It was a world balanced by bravery and bravado. We are cops; we are strong; we handle whatever you put in front of us and ask for more.

As times change, so does departmental policy. Education and outreach have developed crisis teams and peer support within many departments. If this situation were to happen today, that officer would be given peer support, sent home, and would be monitored by a fellow officer and given some sort of counseling. Right or wrong, I was ridiculed for trying to be a "Super Cop" and put right back out on the street. At the time, I didn't think a thing of it. Hell, I was a new guy around there.

Now I know it was the wrong thing for that department to do. I survived it, I was lucky. Now, though, I tell these stories so my brothers and sisters know that their fight is not one they need to wage alone. It is okay to ask for help. I challenge, I beg you to reach out to someone. You may be surprised at how many similar demons people fight daily.

Recently, through some very aggressive prolonged exposure work, I started to recall some intimate details of this one incident. This therapeutic work is difficult but quite amazing. You work through an incident over and over to reduce the intensity of the memory. A born skeptic, I thought this might be a waste of everyone's time. One thing that is really incredible about the therapy, though, are the strange and seemingly insignificant details I began to remember.

For instance, in the train incident, I wore my uniform home that morning. That was quite odd for me. Typically, I would dress at work and then take my uniform off at the end of my shift and bring it home for laundering. That morning, though, I hopped in my Jeep and drove straight home. When I arrived at my house, I removed all my equipment, and immediately threw my uniform in the laundry. That is something I reserved for when I woke up. (What can I say, I like to be fresh?) While these changes in behavior may seem insignificant, they signaled deeper issues.

At the time, I lived alone in a small Cape Cod style house. When I got home that night, after the train incident, I noticed that my answering machine was blinking with one message. A paramedic, a dear friend of mine, had called and left me a message to see if I was okay. "Why does everyone keep asking me this?" I mumbled out loud.

I will say this now to my paramedic friend, "thank you". You have no idea what an impact that one call had on my life.

I sat down in my chair, after listening to my voicemail message, as I always did after work. I turned on the TV and stared at it, as I always did. After a short moment, I caught myself in a day dream. That "short" moment was about 30 minutes long. In that time my mind kept trying to recall the previous evening's events. Something clicked, and like the heavy blanket they put on you for an x-ray, the gravity of what I could remember started to creep into my mind.

Shortly after that evening I had the opportunity to listen to the radio traffic from that evening. Even though they were playing it for me, I heard or was listening to bits and pieces. I was terrified but told no one. I didn't remember 2/3 of any of this. What was wrong with me? I would just smile and shake my head. I started to realize why people kept asking if I was physically okay. Aside from some scrapes, I was physically okay, but I was in mental turmoil.

If you read the reported events, it captures the facts as it should. Officer ran, tackled subject, you know the drill. This is where dispatchers come in. They don't get the reports, they get the raw yelling, screaming, and emotions. When I listened to the recording of the events as they occurred, I sat quietly. I thanked them for playing it back to me and left the dispatch center.

I found the nearest bathroom and, for lack of a better term, lost my shit. I thought about everything I put all those people through that night. The terror of a brother in trouble, maybe dead. I have so much respect for dispatchers. Without them, I would have been in deep trouble many times.

What ensued after the train event were radio interviews, media stories, press conferences, and city commission meetings. I came into work sometime after the incident and found an envelope in my mailbox. The letter said I was being awarded the City of Fargo's Medal of Valor, for risking my life to save another. I try living a humble life, and I really did not want any of that type of attention.

After opening the envelope, I made my way into the locker room. Inside the locker room was one of the officers I respected the most. I had the letter in my hand and told him what it was. He said, "I know. You earned it". I didn't feel that things like this are earned. Fate, luck, bad luck, who can control that? To me, it was like "earning" a case of the flu.

Inside the envelope, I found I had neglected the second piece of paper. It was a summary of events written by the officer who was with me that night. He'd had a front row seat to this incident. As I read what was written, I couldn't believe it. I didn't remember hardly any of the details. Images of that officer standing there after the train passed, flashed through my mind. A flood of emotions went through me all at once. The one emotion that prevailed, was guilt. I felt guilty that all those emergency services had to come to that scene because of me. I felt guilty of what I put that officer through that night. I grabbed that guilty emotion and packed it away for nearly two decades.

It would not be until about 19 years later that I would realize how much that one moment in time, and everything that followed, would change me and my whole perspective on life. With some great guidance, I was able to recall the radio traffic from that evening. Specifically, my officers telling dispatch that the train was so close, they didn't know if I had made it or not. I felt incredibly guilty because that night, those people had a front row seat to what they thought was an officer being killed. There will always probably be gaps for me regarding this incident. But organizing, remembering, apologizing, letting go, has helped me to value saving a life, and being alive.

I am not complaining. I am not looking for sympathy. But I also want people to know that having that paramedic friend call, as seemingly a small gesture as that was, later would save my life. I didn't realize I almost died that day until several years later. Unfortunately for two of my fellow brother's, that call never came for them when they needed it, and I lost them. But that's a whole other story.

That Medal of Valor, well, it was packed away until recently. My angel of a wife told me it was time to display it on a shelf. I didn't know what that meant, but in her wise way, she was telling me, it was time to tell my story. So, there it sits, on the shelf staring at me. But now, I stare right back.

This incident became part of my life and dominated my thoughts. It contributed to unnecessary risk taking and other confusing actions. It became part of my abyss and it was staring me right in the face.

Making that Notification

Most emergency personnel today appear very young to me. Digging through some old photos I found a picture of me as young cop with a flat top haircut. I was standing in my parents' living room in my uniform. I had every accessory known to man on my gun belt. If I were to have fallen in something as shallow as a mud puddle, I surely would have drowned. I looked young too, but inside, I was incredibly old. That moral blanket that protected me as a child, had developed holes like stars in the night sky.

As we get older we tend to submit more to life's plan than when we are young. Dents in our armor act like a shock collar on a dog. When life decides its time, we don't get a trial to plead our case.

This next story is a tough one. Intentionally vague to honor and protect the family, it had a profound impact on my life. Specific details are left out because it is the right thing to do.

Imagine your children are now young adults, making something of themselves. They work. They live at home to save money. As parents, you are walking that empty nester line of being fortunate to have family dinner together and yet wondering if they will ever move out. That perhaps was the case with the family in this incident.

I was called to a business at the beginning of my shift. What I was met with did not seem real to me. This young adult, about my age at the time, had gone to work that evening. At some point during his shift, a freak machine accident had mercilessly taken his life. This scene was gruesome and still plays in my head today. The sights, sounds, smells of that facility became engrained in my senses. Any similar stimulus I receive even now, years later, brings back the memory of that night.

After the scene was processed and deemed not necessarily a police matter, my duty was not over. With the Chaplin, we made our way to notify the family of this tragedy. This was one of the most miserable experiences of my life. As I stood there, I couldn't even tell you what was said. I remember my heart aching for these parents. Here I was, a young man, about the same age as their child, bearing the news a parent never wants to hear. I aged a great deal that evening.

Sometime later I watched the 2009 film "Taking Chance", starring Kevin Bacon and directed by Ross Katz. Kevin Bacon's character's job in the film was to escort his fellow fallen Marine home. Although it was a powerful movie, I know these heroes do exist. It is not the same situation, but the substance of this film brought back the memory of telling those poor parents of their son's death. Another memory that had been pushed as far back in my mental closet as possible.

<u>Been Down This Road Before</u>

I don't know what it is or was, but trouble seemed to follow me like an annoying sibling. Nothing was ever as it seemed while on patrol. Traffic stops turned in to predatory sex offender arrests. Abandoned property turned in to drug warrants. When you thought you had seen just about everything, something new would present itself.

Working the downtown beat was my passion. I loved the action on the weekends. With three major colleges in the metro area, there was bound to be some excitement almost every night. I was doing my evening shift rotation, which overlapped with the night shift. I had been patrolling for three years, making traffic stops, responding to calls, planning when and where to eat.

That evening I saw a car driving about 50 mph and then exit into an alley. The vehicle hit the approach causing it to launch into the air. I quickly caught up with the vehicle, calling out to dispatch the location and direction. The second I turned on my lights, the vehicle veered to the side of the road-way and two occupants jumped out. Like deer being chased by a hunter, they ran in separate directions.

I told you I played a little football in my day. I would never consider a marathon, but for 200 yard runs, you best have running shoes. After 200 yards, my speed that night was like Fruit Stripe gum's flavor, it quickly disappeared.

I was gaining on the driver, yelling "Police Stop!" I was calling out the direction to dispatch of both individuals. The gap between me and the driver closed quickly. To this day, I do not know why, but the driver ran directly down the middle of the street.

A beautiful tackle ended this foot pursuit. A double car had stopped and brought my squad to where I flopped on top of the driver. Handcuffed and searched, we were off to the county jail where the driver was booked on a variety of charges. Another unit had located and arrested the passenger.

I left the jail which was attached to the courthouse. My squad phone rang, so I parked short of the courthouse, facing the parking lot. It was a Sunday, so the lot was typically empty. On the phone was the father of the person I just arrested. He was irate that the police department had arrested his son, but at that point, something caught my attention and his voice was just a soft irritation in my ear.

In the parking lot of the courthouse was a lone vehicle. The irate father on the phone became more of annoyance than he was worth. In the middle of his temper tantrum, I simply hung up.

The court house parking lot sat across the street from the main entrance. A single vehicle with the driver's side door open, sat facing the building. There were two legs hanging out of the vehicle. On the surface, this looked like someone working on stealing a radio out of a car. It was about 6:00 p.m. in summer, so there were at least three hours of light left in the day. I radioed dispatch and told them what I was observing.

The beat officer, my good friend Ezzy, said he would head my way. We rolled up as quietly as we could on this car. As we approached the vehicle, the legs turned into a full figure of a man. He quickly jumped up and sat in the driver's seat of the car.

I said, "Police, what's going on tonight?" The man looked dazed. He mumbled as he spoke, and both of his hands were on the steering wheel. The vehicle appeared as if he had been living in it for some time. Before I could get my next question out, Ezzy yelled "Gun!"

Ezzy grabbed an SKS rifle with a scope from an area within the man's reach. This was an older Volkswagen Beetle, so everything was within his reach. I grabbed the man and put him prone on the ground. He struggled only briefly, but his mumbling and quiet behavior continued. What unraveled next sent chills down my spine.

The man started to speak quietly. He told me that he was mad at a judge because the judge took his knife from him at a court proceeding. The man said he had been sitting in the parking lot, watching, and waiting for the right moment to shoot his way into the building. The man had been watching a Sheriff's Deputy through his rifle scope as the Deputy worked in his office. The man was going to shoot the security guard and anyone that got in his way as he went searching for the judge and his knife. He had been planning this event since the judge had ordered his weapon, a KA-Bar knife, removed from his possession.

Inside this vehicle was a mess of clothes and papers and hundreds of rounds of ammunition for his rifle. There was also some sort of escape and evasion manual. Also, inside the vehicle were galvanized pipes and threaded endcaps consistent with the construction of pipe bombs. There were various nuts and bolts also near the pipe material. The man told me that he had planted pipe bombs around the perimeter of the courthouse. I notified my Sergeant who in turn, notified the newly formed and very local bomb technician squad.

After a cursory search around the courthouse, no pipe bombs were located. The man eventually admitted that he lied about placing the pipe bombs. It was determined that the man was a deserter from the military. He was arrested and taken to the hospital for a mental evaluation.

When Ezzy and I returned to the station. We were both still in amazement that this could have potentially happened in our small city. We did share a morbid, but good laugh at all the planning this man did though. He was going to make his escape in a blaze orange Volkswagen Beetle with green Colorado license plates. No one would have noticed that, of course.

What ensued, again, was a media storm. National news outlets picked up on this story. I was amazed. Ezzy and I were both awarded Meritorious Service Medals from our department.

The County Commission recognized us for being in the right place at the right time. For this incident I am grateful. I am grateful that I was lucky enough to be in the place I was before this act occurred. I am grateful that Ezzy was so close and backed me up. We kept each other safe.

I don't know what demons or memories haunted Ezzy or anyone else at the time. I wish I did. I know, personally, I was focused on taking the highest risk calls and just waiting for the most dangerous situations. I was so wrapped up in life and being a cop. Now looking back, I realize I should have stopped, taken a breath, and looked what was going on around me. But at the time, still reeling from train incidents and potential active shooter situations, I looked forward to any dangerous call within the city.

About a year later, Ezzy took a position with a different department. We would never speak again, nor would I hear that infectious laugh. Several years later, on my birthday, I lost Ezzy. Whatever was haunting him, took him. I should have known. I am sorry I was so blind buddy, I didn't know.

Brother Tim

When my brother said he wanted to do a ride along, I told him that he should wait until it was the weekend. He had ridden with me once before, on a weekday, but it had been a less than exciting evening and weekends usually brought out a more realistic experience of law enforcement.

We made up different identities for my brother as he rode along with me, depending on the type of people we came into contact with during the shift. First, he was just some guy that I picked up alongside the road. Then he was Special Agent Tim of the Undergarment Inspection Service. (You would be surprised how few people questioned that credential.) But by far, my favorite of my brother's personas was Brother Tim, the Bible slinging police car evangelist.

Everyone seemed to love Brother Tim. I really wanted to show Brother Tim the kind of stuff that went on after dark in the downtown area. There was plenty opportunity for Brother Tim to spread the good word, one citizen at a time and this night, Brother Tim would not be disappointed.

Although Fargo is small, cool weekends in the fall are quite active in the downtown area. With the colleges back in session, and football season in full roar, students migrate to the downtown area to celebrate their wins and drown the sorrow of their losses in copious amounts of whatever is on special.

This summer night started out in the briefing room. The swing shift was searching for a person that reportedly brandished a handgun in the downtown area. The report gave a detailed description of the individual. I had logged enough hours downtown to have a pretty good idea of who this mystery person was and where he lived. Other officers working that beat must have come to the same conclusion as they had already knocked on the door of the suspect's pay- by – the-day- or- month apartment door, and had received no answer. The report was that the suspect appeared to be aggressive and walking with no purpose. The complaint also mentioned something about the suspect being "high" or on pain killers.

Brother Tim and I mounted old Squad 83. As in the past, I reminded Brother Tim how to remove the shotgun from the rack if need be. I always felt comfort when someone who knew how to effectively use the shot gun was sitting next to me in the squad car. Brother Tim was no exception. He had years of bird hunting under his belt with that very brand of shotgun.

We started checking local areas where we thought the suspect may be hanging out or hiding.

Another officer was placed about a block north of the suspect's downtown apartment building to conduct surveillance. This was a difficult task as it was dark, the weekend, and downtown was alive with traffic and crowds standing around talking and bar hopping.

More reports of an individual matching a similar description started coming in from all areas adjacent to the downtown area. We checked out every reported sighting with no success.

The swing shift beat officer and I decided to search a large apartment building near the residence of our suspect. The building was rather iconic. If you worked downtown, you could bet you would be called to this building at least once a shift. On cold nights, transients would sneak into the basement where it was warm and sleep off whatever was ailing them. It seemed logical that this would be a place to at least eliminate as a potential hiding place.

Brother Tim, dressed as a civilian, posted in the public hallway of the main floor.

The swing shift officer and I started searching in the basement. Some basements are pure dungeon. The stairs for this basement looked like you were descending into hell. This basement was a dungeon. Flashlights beaming, we searched corner to corner. Surprisingly, no transients and no suspect were there. Just a bunch of old clothes. We made our way back up to Brother Tim.

The building consisted of five floors. On the main floor, there was a business office. The owner, who was well known to officers, maintained his residence in the building. The rest of the building had a variety of apartments and a cast of characters whose nightly performances kept the beat officers busy. The owner was known for giving those who were struggling, a chance. The owner often allowed certain tenants lower rent rates and flexible terms. Some residents of the building were down on their luck, others had legal troubles. Some residents just lived there because of the convenience of downtown.

We climbed the stairs of the building, searching stairwells and the resident floors. On most nights, you could hear music, yelling, and partying. But on this night, it was the quietest I had ever heard this building. It was a weird feeling.

Standing in one of the stairwells, the beat officer, Brother Tim, and I were contemplating our next move. The stairwells in this old brick building were wide. Because of the concrete and brick, sounds were amplified. When someone spoke, the sound echoed off the concrete floors and walls, looking for somewhere to escape.

Brother Tim said that he could hear running water. I also could hear it and had never heard that noise before in this building. It wasn't like water gushing onto a floor, more like running through pipes at a rapid rate. The sound of running water has a profound effect on me. In law enforcement, if there is an opportunity to take a bathroom break, it should be taken. I thought it would be a good time to run back to the station and take a bathroom break so we left the building certain our suspect was not there.

Whether you are a cop, a farmer, doctor, or homemaker, things tend to get routine. Small but obvious indicators or stimuli can unintentionally be overlooked. I am not speaking about blood on the wall or shoe prints leaving a burglary scene. I am referring more to faint sounds, smells, or just something that you can't quite place or put into perspective enough to come to any sort of conclusion. Because these indicators can seem harmless at the time, they are typically noted but not acted upon. In hindsight, these indicators can reveal a great deal of what was occurring at the time.

"Man do I feel better," I told Brother Tim, after the bathroom break. We got back in squad 83 and headed westbound towards the action of Broadway. A sudden chirp of the radio and the voice of the officer on surveillance broke the silence. The officer indicated that an individual matching the suspect's description was walking southbound on Broadway, which also happened to be right in front of where the apartment of the suspect was situated.

I pulled my squad car up slowly so I could just make out the sidewalk on the corner that met with Broadway. I told Brother Tim to stay in the car, unless notified. I also reminded him of how to get the shotgun out in case my ass needed saving. I decided to make the rest of the corner on foot, instead of in the car. I left about half of the car exposed in case I needed to get back to it for cover.

There were several people walking up and down the sidewalk. I made my way around the corner where there were more people and cars slowly cruising up and down the street. I was about a half of a block south of the suspect's apartment and I scanned for the suspect. "If I have to shoot, this is going to be really tough", I thought to myself. So many people and cars.

Bingo! There is the suspect. "Mmmmm hmmmm" I said to myself, as I realized it was exactly who I thought it was. I started snaking my way toward the suspect. The suspect was about 150 feet away, walking slowly and directly to me. The pedestrians on the sidewalk provided excellent concealment.

In my ears, I can hear my heart beating like a drum. I told dispatch I was going to be out with a suspect matching the description from the earlier complaint. As I walked toward the suspect, still concealed by the sidewalk traffic, I kept trying to formulate a plan in my head to keep them from becoming victims if I had to exchange gun fire with this person.

It was clear to me that the suspect had not seen me yet. 50 feet now. I had a clear view of his hands, waist, and head. A million thoughts race through my head. I reminded myself, even though I know this person, he is a suspect and safety is paramount.

Then, as luck would have it, a familiar face. A local resident I had known since the day I started in law enforcement, was standing on the street corner. I motioned to the resident in the direction of the suspect. The resident confirmed the suspect's name.

Doing a little Monday morning quarterbacking, what I did next, I may or may not do differently today. So, what would you do? Some would draw their weapon and charge. Others would wait for back up to arrive on the scene, and some may not do anything and wait for the young officer to get there to deal with the suspect.

The interesting thing with law enforcement is there is a "right", where the majority hope we live and a "wrong" of which we try to avoid. And then there is that subjective ground in the middle where there is really no definite right or wrong and where doing the right thing may still be wrong and vice versa. In a world of perception versus reality, it is a daily balancing act where the goal is survival and the upholding of the oath which was taken on the first day we became an officer. That is where we live. The details of each circumstance, although they may appear similar, can be quite different than the next.

I had dealt with this person a few times in the past. I would not say it was all positive, but the suspect knew who I was. It would not be out of character for me to approach him like any other day.

With a crowded street, vehicles slowly rolling by and other officers rapidly approaching, I decided to conduct what is call a "Terry Stop", or otherwise known as a "Stop and Frisk". Police may conduct a Terry Stop when they have a reasonable suspicion that an individual is armed, engaged in criminal conduct, or about to be engaged in criminal conduct. At this point, the officer may briefly stop and detain an individual for a pat-down search of outer clothing. The Fourth Amendment considers a Terry Stop a seizure.

Ten feet now is all that separated me from the suspect. I came in from an angle to his left shoulder. "Hey there. Police. What's your name?"

The suspect stopped dead in his tracks. What the suspect did not know was that my weapon was at the ready alongside my right leg. Pedestrians seemed now to steer wide of this pending confrontation between the young police officer and the suspect. The suspect mumbled his name, and now I had that confirmation. Like a statue, the suspect kept their hands motionless.

"You have any weapons on you?" No answer, just a blank stare from his glossy eyes.

Like in old western movies when two people meet in the street because one had been called out, the pedestrians scattered into nooks, crannies, alleys. It must have been apparent to everyone standing around that there was about to be some sort of enforcement action.

Just then, I see another officer moving quickly on foot directly behind the suspect. I would have to move one way or the other should I need to engage this person. "Mind if I check?" I said. Again, no answer, but instead, a reaction. I slowly moved to the suspect's blind spot and holstered.

Slowly, the suspect raised his hands straight in the air. As the shirt raised from the belt line an undeniable shine of a large hand gun presented itself. The suspect started to turn

"Gun!" I yelled. I don't remember which of the department- approved take down techniques I applied, but it worked well. He ended up face down, hands out on the sidewalk with my knee in his upper back. The other officer ended up in the same position, on the other side of the suspect.

"Knife!" the other officer yelled. The suspect also had a large butcher knife concealed in the small of his back. I handcuffed the suspect just as two more squads and the shift sergeant pulled up on the scene.

A crowd gathered across the street, watching the activity. The suspect was not answering any questions. Another officer took the shiny 1911 .45 handgun and knife and secured them. The shift sergeant and I began to search the suspect. The suspects pockets were full of everything imaginable. With the suspect still on the ground, I started removing what seemed like an endless amount of change from his pocket. Then a pair of Rolex watches, keys, pills, and a driver's license.

The door of the nearest squad car was open, and I could hear the familiar tones that indicated the fire department was going to be dispatched to the apartment building that the beat officer, Brother Tim and I had searched earlier that evening. I saw the trucks cross Broadway and park. One of the fireman radioed that there was an active fire in one of the apartments, but the door would not open.

The shift sergeant and I were still removing items from the suspects pockets, questioning where this individual would get a pair of Rolex watches. Then we found something that changed everything. A wallet, which after searching through it, clearly didn't belong to the suspect. Inside the wallet was the driver's license of the apartment building owner. The same apartment building we had previously searched.

My shift sergeant and I locked eyes and he grabbed for his shoulder microphone. We did not have a direct radio link to the fire department, so dispatch had to relay messages. My shift sergeant asked dispatch to confirm what apartment the fire department was at. It was confirmed. The building owner's apartment was on fire.

"The water!" I said. "That was it! Brother Tim heard water rushing through pipes in the building. It was the sprinkler system to suppress a fire!" My shift sergeant told dispatch to have the fire department force the door into the apartment, and they did.

The suspect was taken to the emergency room by officers and detectives. I went back to my squad car where a wide-eyed Brother Tim was sitting, having watched all of this unfold. I told Brother Tim a synopsis of what had happened and what may be to follow the rest of the evening.

I pulled my car around to the avenue side of the apartment building. The fire department appeared to have contained and exterminated the blaze. It was confirmed what we had suspected. The building owner did not survive what appeared to be robbery, murder, and arson. We needed to establish our perimeter, and the real work was about to begin.

I stood outside the car with my shift sergeant and Brother Tim. Brother Tim said, "Well, I should probably go so you guys can work." The shift sergeant handed Brother Tim a roll of crime scene tape and requested he make a tape barrier. Brother Tim grinned from ear to ear. I watched as a fellow officer solemnly approached the family of the building owner. I knew what was happening and said a little prayer under my breath for all of them.

I was summoned back to the police department. Brother Tim had a drive ahead of him, so he called it a night. I met with a detective to assist with an affidavit for a search warrant. Ultimately, the suspect was charged, pleaded guilty, and if not dead, is in prison to this day. As for Brother Tim, that was the last ride along he would ever do. I don't know if I ever told Brother Tim how important that one observation he made was in this case. I will say this, when it comes to crime scene tape, nobody beats Brother Tim.

Lucky Catch

Luck is abstract. Some may also say that about religion. Regardless of your beliefs, you cannot deny that sometimes you are just in the right place at the right time. The only question at that point is why you were put in that situation. Maybe it was luck, fate perhaps, or God's will. Regardless of belief, we are placed in situations and find we have to participate. Instead of watching the play, life assigns us a role. Sometimes your character is Pedestrian #3, and sometimes you may be singing the lead in Oklahoma.

Working the nightshift downtown, officers would often patrol in a square eight blocks by fourteen blocks. The amount of calls in that one area could far surpass some of the larger beats in the city. Being a beat officer was very effective in a city this size. Officers could recognize things that seemed harmlessly out of place.

On this particular night, it was dark-- inky black. I was southbound on North University Drive. Glancing to my right I noticed a vehicle with its parking lights on. The interior light was also on, but I could not make out what was going on inside. The parking lot surrounded an old building that contained businesses that were only open on typical weekdays and hours.

This vehicle was out of place, so I made a hard right and drove slowly past. I could see that the person in the driver's seat was looking behind into the backseat area. As I drove by, he turned and our eyes met. You may hear a lot about a sixth sense, gut feelings, or another undefined stimulus. This was an occasion where something was definitely off. I could feel it, but I couldn't define it. I proceeded past the vehicle, giving the driver my best cop stare.

Once past the parking lot, I shot around the block for a second look. When I reached North University Drive for the second time, the vehicle was pulling out of the parking lot.

North University Drive was a one way heading south, and this vehicle had nowhere to go but that direction. As the vehicle exited the parking lot, it did not engage its headlights, thankfully, so it gave me a reason to stop it. The vehicle turned sharply south, about a half block in front of me. I turned on my overhead lights and the vehicle immediately pulled over. I could now see three heads in the vehicle. They remained motionless.

Our department did a very good job of backing each other up on traffic stops. We constantly monitored the radio and if another unit was on a stop, we did our best to get there to back them up until the end of the stop. It must have been a slow night, as I had a couple squads come to back me.

I approached the vehicle and noticed that the driver was a male, and there were two younger passengers, maybe 14 years old, in the back seat. The driver produced a license of which I had dispatch run. He seemed extremely nervous. Typically, we take the license back to the car and run it through our vehicle computer, but I wanted to stay engaged with this individual as I now had my eyes on him.

My senses perked up when dispatch came back with, "314 HQ." "Go ahead" I responded. "Are you 104?" they asked. "Am I 104? Yes, yes, I am 104." This is a question our dispatch asked when you have a subject with a warrant, protection order, or other document placed into the National Crime Information Center (NCIC) or the state system known as CWIS. I told the driver to step out of the vehicle and place his hands on the door frame of the vehicle. "10-4, go ahead".

I was informed that the driver of the vehicle was on parole for sex offenses. The two children in the back seat stated they did not know this person. They would not say exactly how they met the driver of the vehicle. The driver's parole officer contacted me via my squad cell phone. He requested I arrest the driver based on the totality of the circumstances I described. Another officer took custody of the juveniles and reunited them with their parents.

I called for a hook, our slang name for a tow truck, and began to search the subject's vehicle. There was some alcohol containers and candy wrappers strewn about the interior of the vehicle. I grabbed the keys and walked around to the rear of the vehicle. After a quick twist of the key, the trunk lid popped open. I was horrified at what was found in that trunk. Video games, stuffed animals, toys, candy, soda. It looked like a mobile county fair. Based on the whole story that had unraveled before me I could only believe these seemingly harmless items had only one terrible purpose.

Sometime later, I traveled with the parole officer to a prison in Minneapolis, MN. I was called to testify at the parole revocation hearing. Upon my testimony, the subject's parole was revoked and he was placed back into the custody of the Minnesota Department of Corrections.

That dark night on University Avenue proved to be a good night for me and for the unsuspecting children who were spared the possible horrors that car's driver represented.

The Unexpected

Some of the closest calls I ever have had were completely spontaneous and at the end of my shift. As the downtown beat officer, I spent a great deal of time at the emergency room situated on my beat. Injury accidents, rape victims, or drunk driver blood draws, the "ER" was always a hub of activity. I developed close relationships with the staff of the ER.

One day I had responded to an injury accident on the west edge of the downtown beat.   The person's injuries were concerning enough that they earned a ride in an ambulance to the ER. I was able to process the majority of the accident, with the exception of an account from the injured individual. As I had many times in the past, I made my way to the ER to speak with the injured party, hoping to collect details of the accident.

I had been recently "rewarded" by being moved to the day shift. I hated day shift. Shoplifters, traffic accidents, and brass around the station all day long.

What most people do not realize about North Dakota is that the summers can be quite hot and humid. Any area that has water becomes a perfect breeding habitat for mosquitos. Our uniforms were black, uncomfortable, and exceptionally hot. I had graduated from bike patrol school earlier that spring with the sole purpose of being allowed to wear shorts while working. I never once rode a bicycle on a shift.

On the day of this accident, I entered the ER and was welcomed by the familiar faces of the doctors and nurses attending to patients. The staff at the ER were familiar with seeing me walk through restricted areas. The ER was essentially a large circle of rooms for patient treatment. In the center of the circle was the nurse's station, ambulance desk, and the doctors' workspace. I greeted the familiar faces and headed to my accident victim's room. It was unusually busy for 5:15 p.m.

The injuries sustained from the crash did not prevent the victim from providing his account of the accident. I completed the required forms and started to make my way back around the circle of treatment rooms. I was walking past the last room prior to exiting the large circle and briefly glanced into the last room.

Inside the room was a large, very belligerent Native American man of whom I had dealt with on numerous occasions. I remember him from my time working at the jail. When I was a deputy, he had been arrested for disorderly conduct and had gold paint all over his face.

I found out later that the ambulance had come across this male lying on the ground with several abrasions. He was apparently intoxicated and had attempted to ride a bicycle down an underpass. The concrete got the best of him. Since the ambulance had brought him to the ER, he had not been searched for weapons. I would find this out quickly as his eyes met mine. He had a fire in his eyes and was very hostile. Standing about 6 foot 4 and well over 300 pounds, he was a big man.

"You're here for me aren't you, asshole!" He screamed at me.

I assured him I was not. At that moment, he produced a knife and held it toward my direction. As he drew his knife, I instantly drew my gun. My back was literally to the inner circle wall. The medical staff ran out of the room and an unarmed security guard flanked me on the left. My heart began to thump hard in my chest, keeping time in both of my ears.

I knew from several trips inside the ER that my portable radio was completely useless in the confines of the facility. In order to communicate with anyone, we typically went to the ambulance desk and called dispatch. I told the security guard to call 911 and tell them 114 was in a standoff with an armed male.

The medical staff at this facility was and is first class. They immediately began clearing patients as far away from this stand- off situation as possible.

"Richard, put that knife down right now. You are scaring people in here!" I said forcefully.

He refused to comply.

I could see the knife wasn't huge, but it could definitely deliver fatal blows, especially considering his size and strength. He swayed back and forth, "Fuck you, asshole!" he yelled. He held the knife in his left hand, bent elbow, and at waist level. He had not taken a step forward, only side to side, catching himself from falling from the effects of the alcohol.

For those of you who have been cops, you have probably heard of the 21-foot rule. The theory behind this rule is that someone armed with a knife will be able to stab you several times, perhaps fatally, before you could engage them with your firearm if they are 21 feet or closer to you. I was fairly confident that Richard's current level of intoxication would prevent him from moving with any cat -like swiftness towards me. Nonetheless, I was not playing. I had to protect not only myself, but the people in this ER. My firearm was out, and I was aimed in, center mass.

"Richard, you need to put that knife down, I am not here for you," I exclaimed.

Richard didn't answer. He was backed up to the wall in the room and my back was against the wall in the hallway. In my head, my inner voice chimed in. "This is it, this is happening, you are going to have to shoot this guy".

"Put it down Richard!" Faster and faster, thump, thump, thump, in my ears.

Then another voice, not the one in my head, but a voice coming from the ground near the doctor's work station. It sounded like a forceful whisper. "Shoot the fucker" the voice said. "He is in an ER, he won't die!" the voice continued. I considered it as this seemed inevitable. I didn't take my eyes off Richard, but I recognized the voice as one of the medical staff at the ER. Furthermore, he did have somewhat of a valid point.

It felt like a lifetime had passed and I do not remember all of the unpleasant conversation that Richard and I were having, but here we were, no closer to a resolution than when this started. Richard took a step forward. I estimated he was about twenty feet directly in front of me at this point. Thump, thump, thump, in my ears. "Don't do this Richard!" I yelled. I also started to squeeze. Slowly, I leveled my sights of my Glock in the center of Richard's face. We were trained to press, not squeeze the trigger. Thump, thump, thump, my heart started to beat in time with my breath. I began my trigger press. *Goodbye Richard, my center mass target is the level with your eyes and my trigger press is halfway there. This is it.*

"Richard, if you take one more step, I am going to fucking kill you!" I yelled. I squeezed and waited for the slack to give into the rear-ward motion of the trigger, followed by a violent explosion. This is the worst.

Like an alarm clock waking you from a nightmare, Richard's eyes widened, and I could tell he knew I had every intention of following through with what I had said. He looked at me and took a step back. Suddenly, Richard raised the knife, and pointed it to his own throat. That voice in my head exclaimed, "Well that's a step in the right direction."

What seemed like a lifetime had passed.

Suddenly, the cavalry arrived. I don't know where they all came from, but a sea of police officers surrounded me, pushing me back. I holstered my Glock, and I was exhausted. I was pushed to the back of the crowd where I could hear one of the officers, a trained negotiator, was able to convince Richard to put the knife down. He was ultimately arrested for Terrorizing, a Class C Felony in the North Dakota Century Code. My work was done there. I left and went home.

That young security guard was sharp. He manipulated the surveillance camera to capture the event as it unfolded. They provided me a copy. I watched it only once. I didn't need to relive that moment any more than that. That security guard later applied to the police department and became a great police officer. I was grateful to be surrounded by such a competent staff that day.

I didn't sleep that night. The images of Richards forehead in my Glock's front sight remained. I laid in bed, staring at the ceiling listening to my heart beat, thump, thump thump.

Football Season

I am an alumnus of the North Dakota State University, home of the Bison. NFL greats such as Phil Hanson, Tyrone Braxton, and Carson Wentz graced the turf at this land-grant institution. As a child I dreamed of playing football for NDSU. NDSU was a Division II powerhouse. The pitch option offense led by Jeff Bentrim kept you on the edge of your seat the entire game. Ed Shultz was the very vocal and opinionated commentator. At one game at Dacotah Field, someone threw a whiskey bottle into the broadcast booth. That is North Dakota football.

Ed Shultz went on to become a liberal talk radio personality on MSNBC and with some Russian media outlet. A record setting quarterback himself, he provided animated and detailed commentary during Bison football games. He passed away in 2018. Coaches came and went. Football season and the people who gave the color commentary and directed the players, and the players themselves provided much entertainment for eager audiences.

As a police officer, we sometimes had issues with football players. House parties combined with a little liquid courage often resulted in calls to uncooperative coaches defending their players' actions. The program was starting to suffer at one point, because of these issues. Officer's told stories of a particular coach that was extremely vocal with police, spitting tobacco "accidently" in the officers direction as he yelled and screamed like a professional wrestling manager.

If the program was going to grow, NDSU would need to focus on accountability. They selected a new coach who certainly instilled accountability in his players. When we were called to house parties and did not receive cooperation, he partnered with us to bring these types of behaviors into check.

One night at a known college party house, many of the football players were holed up inside. When we first arrived, the music thumped the ground. Windows were open and the smell of stale keg beer and urine penetrated the air.

"Man, I missed college," I thought to myself.

When we arrived at the party house, there was little cooperation. Whoever was inside refused to answer the door. I am surprised the house didn't collapse with the amount of people inside. I wondered how they kept everyone so quiet.

A call was placed to the coach at the time. Waking up a coach at 3:00 a.m. on a Sunday is ill- advised. When the coach arrived, he was apologetic and requested to speak with those inside. When the temporary tenants saw who was standing next to us, the door opened and the party dispersed, with the exception of those players identified by the coach.

The speech that followed would rival any coach's motivational words prior to a state championship game. He didn't yell but spoke very matter-of-fact.

"Did you all have a good time tonight?" he asked.

There is always one in the group that answers that question with a "yes".

"That's great, but I want you to get rested up because come Monday, we will be conducting some conditioning drills to improve our performance." I respect coaches that follow through, and from what I heard, he most certainly did. I respected him because he was not mainstream and made a conscious effort to do the right thing. I know he ended up coaching in the NFL and they were lucky to have him.

Eligibility

As the city of Fargo grew, so did NDSU. The college
made their transition to Division I. That meant the stakes got
higher. The recruiting of bigger, faster, stronger players was
relentless. I would like to stress the word "bigger". Some of
these kids were 18 and 19 years old and stood well over 6' 6".
Most topped the scales at well over 300 pounds. I still wonder
sometimes what they were feeding some of these kids.

While dealing with some of these gigantic humans, I had
to remind myself that even though they were huge, they were
still kids. With football season just starting and college in its first
week, the calls for service increased during the afternoon and
night shifts. One perfect evening, a cool breeze filled the air
with the smell of backyard barbeques and campfires. I was
working Beat 13 that covered the area surrounding the campus. I
loved this time of year.

"213 HQ" dispatch called. I quickly answered with the
anticipation of a possible Sorority out of control or people
streaking down 12th Avenue.

*"Attempt to locate a large, white male yelling and
throwing beer bottles at cars and other people on their porches"*
the call rang out. I was about a block away from the complaint.

I parked my car at the end of the block and started walking
northbound toward campus.

He wasn't hard to find. People were pointing at him as I
walked quickly in his direction. He was the size of a tree and I
was still 30 yards behind him. He was wearing shorts and no
shoes walking on the sidewalk. He was yelling and throwing
glass bottles of beer at cars and at people sitting in front of their
homes. I picked up my pace and went into intercept mode. I
heard the radio call out that at least two more squads were
headed my way, including the campus police. As I got within 10
yards of this massive human, he turned around and saw me. The
race was on and I had the clear speed advantage.

"Police! Stop!" I yelled.

That mountain of a human took off running like an
elephant from a group of photographers on a safari. *"HQ 213 in
a foot pursuit northbound University. White male. Shorts. No
shoes"* I huffed as I ran after the huge human. He turned to go in
between two houses. I saw emergency lights coming my way
and knew my help would be here shortly.

When people run from the police, obviously there is a
reason. If you are going to run from the police, make sure you
can outrun them. Don't be a 325-pound drunk white guy
wearing board shorts and no shoes.

When the suspect sprinted to the rear of the house, he turned to see if he had lost me. He had not; I was right on him. It was dusk and light still emitted through the trees. He looked forward, and then turned to check where I was, but that would be the last time. I had already left my feet and was airborne. I hit him hard in the upper part of his back with my shoulder. He flew off the ground and landed with a thud. A squad car's front bumper stopped inches from his forehead. The officer in the squad car stepped out and stood there for a second with his mouth wide open. From his vantage point, I had just form tackled a guy the size of a building. What I didn't share until later was what really happened.

Timing is everything. Combined with a little luck, an illusion can be created and make anyone witnessing an event believe they saw something that didn't happen. A good magician can make a trick look as if the impossible is possible. I was not a magician, but my timing was perfect that night. Everything regarding the foot pursuit was absolutely true. What I did not share was how Mother Nature helped me out that night. At the same moment my shoulder contacted the massive human, he tripped over a 2 foot ledge of compacted dirt in the alley. I am sure to someone watching this, it would look as if this short cop laid out some crazy NFL form tackle on a wide receiver, but that was not the case.

I had to use two sets of handcuffs on the guy. I found out he was only 19 years old and was merely a prospect football player. The ride to the jail was interesting. He was a definite shit talker. He was confused as everyone else how someone my size could lay out a huge guy. When he got a good look at me in the alley by the jail, it didn't get any better. He refused to believe that I was able to hit him so hard that he landed on the ground, knocking the wind out of him. The trash talk continued into the booking room.

Booking rooms are amazing places. Countless times, I have put up with verbal abuse, threats, promises of bodily harm to me and my family, only to have the person I arrested change their attitude completely while standing in front of that booking counter. What really seemed to get people the most was the call to mom. This massive lug was no different. All of the anger, threats, and hostility ended when his Mother answered at the other end of the phone. This massive child, who minutes before said he could tear me apart, was reduced to someone a Teletubby could bully.

The simple sound of his Mother's voice changed everything. I felt bad for his mom. It had to have been tough to get that call. The coach later spoke with another officer and asked him if I had any years of college eligibility left to play football. The funny thing was that I indeed did have two years left, but no intention of going back. He should have given that offer to the mound of dirt the prospective player tripped over while running from the police.

Door Ding

On a rare occasion, my wife would ride with me. There was always an interesting phenomenon that would occur whenever she was riding during the shift. There was not one time where we didn't encounter a naked person. I don't know how or why, but she was a magnet for the people wanting to display their flesh. The time of day did not seem to matter.

Around 7:00 p.m. on one ride along, we were dispatched to a shirtless man who appeared intoxicated, walking down a very busy Main Avenue. My partner Ezzy was dispatched as back up to the call. I quickly spotted the man stumbling down the center of the very busy four lane road. It was just getting dark but there was still enough light to keep the street light from illuminating the surrounding area. Cars whizzed by left and right. The man swore and gestured to drivers honking and yelling at him to get out of the way.

I pulled up at an angle and turned my emergency lights on. I could hear them grinding as they rotated. The lights danced across the man's face. I had never seen him before. Ezzy pulled up also and together we approached the man.

The fight was on before we even got a word out. All three of us ended up on our sides by the passenger door of my car. The man smelled of body odor, booze and was slippery with sweat. It was hard to get a handle on him. From the passenger seat of my squad car, my wife was watching Ezzy and I try to capture this slick skinned drunk. At some point the man ended up on his hands and knees with Ezzy and me grabbing at his gross and sweaty form.

"Stop resisting!" I repeated over and over.

"I will fucking kill you guys!" he screamed. The man was thrashing around like someone receiving a terrible shock. He was obviously drunk and angry at something. After nearly being hit by several cars, we had to get him off the street.

Apparently, my wife had seen enough and was eager to help. As the subject tried to stand from his position on all fours, he raised his head towards the passenger side of my car. Without warning, my wife threw the door opened and exited to assist us. The door impacted the man's head with a loud thud. The fight was over.

"He said he was going to kill you guys and I wanted to help you" my wife said. The man laid on the ground, grabbing his forehead. He was fine, and it sure took the fight out of him. He didn't say a word on the way to jail. When he was finally booked, he turned and said to my wife, "That hurt you bitch" and was led to his cell. I am sure it did hurt.

<u>No Pants, Out of Service</u>

I have a passion for animals. I can not stand to watch one more ASPCA commercial accompanied by Sara McLaughlin singing "Arms of an Angel". Those wide-eyed, shaking dogs do me in every single time. I actually have had a much easier time dealing with human suffering than with animal suffering. I feel as humans we have much more control over our environment than animals.

We had animal control officers that worked primarily day and early swing shifts. This became quite a luxury for officers who worked those shifts. The night shift was rarely fortunate enough to have a trained animal control officer. We were responsible for the safe apprehension, transport, and booking of whatever creature with which we were dealing. I had been called to traditional cats in a tree, lost dogs, and two bats that had collided and got stuck to one another. I did not care for animal calls because we rarely dealt with animals that were not in some sort of distress.

For some reason, most of the animals hated me.

Working on a hot July night, I was dispatched to a large bank parking lot in the heart of the city. Dispatch informed me that someone witnessed a dog locked in a hot car. It was a hot night, probably about 96 degrees with 80 percent humidity. This type of weather did not suit me or my polyester uniform well at all. I rolled up to the bank parking lot and located the single vehicle exactly where the caller described it would be parked. I turned on my spotlight and could clearly see that there was a large German Shepard sitting in the rear seat. The German Shepard looked like a passenger just waiting for its driver. *How horrible*, I thought as I approached the vehicle and tried the doors on the driver's side. Both doors were locked, and the windows were up.

Because it was so hot, and the vehicle was not running, I considered smashing a window. This was a big German Shepard. "Hang in there buddy!" I said, as if the dog knew what I was saying. The dog did not like what I was doing. In short, he was pissed. He growled and snapped at the window. "Hey, settle down partner, I am trying to help you," I pleaded. The dog continued to bark and growl at me as if I were trying to harm him. I picked up my shoulder microphone to call a supervisor. I noticed a little detail I had initially missed upon my approach to the vehicle.

As far as I could tell, the vehicle appeared secure. The exception was the rear passenger window, which was all the way down. In a flash, this 85-pound animal of muscle and teeth was out the window!

I ran towards the open door of my car. My right foot made it into the squad, but not before this beast of a dog's teeth took hold of my delicate polyester uniform pants. With one violent shake, I was left standing with what could be considered, no pants. If I was a citizen downtown, an arrest for indecent exposure would have been imminent. This dog had, with surgical precision, removed 80 percent of my pants.

As I stood there in shock wearing only my uniform top, gun belt and boots, I made my move. I jumped into the car and watched the German Shepard enjoy destroying what was left of my pants. I was safe in my car, and boy did the air conditioning feel good when you don't have any pants on. There had been many naked and pant less persons in my police car, it had just never been me. I was hoping that the surveillance cameras at the bank did not capture this fiasco. The hard part would be trying to phrase this to dispatch as I would need to travel back to the station for a fresh set of trousers.

"HQ, ahhh 314" I called on my radio.

"Go ahead" the dispatcher responded

"Ya, I am going to be 10-6 for a bit"

Then I laughed, yes, "bit" indeed. "I had a little fight with a dog and will need some seamstress assistance."

I could hear the dispatcher covering her laughter when she approved my request. I took the humiliating, and drafty, drive back to the station. When I arrived, it would be a safe bet that all eyes in the dispatch center were on the surveillance

camera affixed above the heavy steel door that led to the station.
I quickly made my way down the stairs. I found my locker and
made myself whole again.

There was an audible giggle from the dispatchers any
time my beat number was called for some time after this
incident.

Mother Knows Best

If you can ever find a law enforcement officer willing to
schedule you for a ride along, I recommend that you do it. It may
be a slow shift, or it may be an eye-opening experience. It is
sometimes difficult when a family member rides with officers,
however. There are inherent dangers of which they can be
exposed. There are certain restraints a person must follow when
you have a belligerent drunk in the rear of your car, for example.
When there is a family member riding with you and an
intoxicated person's colorful language becomes directed at that
family member, it is only natural to take that behavior a bit more
personal.

I was working day shift and my mom decided it was
time to do a ride along. I picked a day where we would maybe
have a shoplifter or some traffic accidents to deal with. The
dangers of the job were obvious but having my mother in the car

put my shift under a microscope. I wanted to show her that not every call involved a life or death struggle.

At the time of my mother's ride-a-long, the city had experienced a rash of church burglaries in recent days. Undercover police officers were even given overtime to surveil potential target locations. On that day of the ride-a-long, dispatch sent us to a house on the eastern portion of my beat. The Mother of a juvenile teenager called dispatch and reported she thought her son had acquired some property that did not belong to him.

When we arrived at the home, the Mother escorted me to her basement. There was a variety of musical instruments and sound equipment. The woman said there was no way her son would be able to purchase all of this equipment. Furthermore, the equipment had the name of the church stamped all over each piece. This is what we call a clue.

The woman led me to her son. He was about sixteen and rather disrespectful. In the business, I would describe him to other officers as a "mouthpiece". There was clearly probable cause for an arrest. Since he was a juvenile and it was a felony level amount of equipment, we would bypass Attendant Care and go straight to Juvenile Detention. "Attendant Care" was basically a room with an adult that supervised juveniles that were charged with low level offenses or even runaways. I walked to my squad car and told my mother a little about what was going on with the call.

I placed handcuffs on the juvenile and placed him in the rear of my squad car. My mother was sitting in the passenger seat. I walked back about 20 feet from my car and was speaking with the juvenile's Mother. She was remorseful and somewhat emotionally hurt. I turned around to check on my mother and noticed that she was unbelted, turned around, and facing the juvenile. I can not say for sure, but I believe she was reinforcing what ever she was saying with a pointed finger.

"Who is that?" The woman asked.

"Well, that's my mother and by the looks of it she is making a point to your son." I replied.

"Good!" the woman said, turned and walked back into her house. I waited until my mother had turned back around in her seat. I wanted nothing to do with that lecture.

When I shut the car door, it was as quiet as a cold winter night. No cussing, swearing, or disrespectful behavior. There were a long series of small sobs coming from the back seat of my squad car. I looked over at my mother who was staring straight ahead. She turned towards me with a smile and we took our little felon to juvenile detention. It could only get easier for him from there.

<h2 style="text-align:center"><u>The Run Down</u></h2>

Most police officers have the ability to hold a conversation, drive, monitor the radio and scanner all the same time. Multitasking is an important part of the job in any emergency service occupation. If a police officer is not listening to the radio, critical information regarding those around you can be missed. It takes practice and discipline to multitask, be accurate, and be efficient. An officer does not want to have to wait for dispatch to provide them information when they could act even seconds sooner.

It was a clear night in Fargo, North Dakota. I was a night shift officer and had just come on shift. There was typically a two to three hour overlap from the power shift so that we could keep as many officers on the street as possible. Just before, during, and two hours after bar closing, the calls would come pouring into the dispatch center. Aside from the usual car accident and traffic stops, it had been a relatively quiet night so far. It had rained just enough to keep the grass about as wet as a morning dew. The moon and stars had started to poke through the clouds in the sky.

I was in a single officer car just leaving the Central Garage area. The Central Garage was located on Beat 13. It was a medium sized beat that included industrial, one of the largest colleges in the state, and one of the higher crime rate neighborhoods. The silence of the radio was suddenly broken by an officer's desperate call for help.

The officer was on foot at a call. I do not know the circumstances of why the officer ended up on the ground, but a suspect got into a vehicle and attempted to run him over.

The call for help from a fellow police officer is one you never want to hear. The officer was able to give a description of the vehicle. Tearing out of the parking lot, I headed to the general area where this vehicle had sped away. My heart was racing and my motor roared towards Main Avenue.

There it was, just as described by the officer. The radio was wild with traffic. The shift Sergeant was able to maneuver behind the vehicle and give chase. As they flew in front of me, another squad car joined my side and three of us gave chase to the suspect.

The vehicle was moving fast, but so were we. There was no way in hell this person was getting away. He tried to kill one of my brothers and we were catching him.

There are so many things to consider when pursuing someone in a vehicle. Add weather conditions, other traffic, a metro area, and pedestrians, the dynamics change every second. Applying all of these and more factors, you can almost guarantee that a violation of the Department Pursuit Policy was in your future. In this case, we needed to get this person before they killed someone. We sped down a major street easily tripling the posted speed limit. The sight must have looked something like how the Blue Angels fly in their formation. Lights, siren, other vehicles all jumbled together in a hot pursuit. This was dangerous.

The trio of cars was approximately 150 feet off the target vehicle's bumper. I could smell my brakes as they heated from having to prevent a collision with the other squad cars. The target vehicle had a choice to head east or west. East would enter an apartment and trailer park community. West would head to a T-intersection and if missed, would dead end into the interstate fence. The vehicle chose west. We backed off more.

The police lights illuminated all the surrounding buildings with red, white, and blue flashes. As the target vehicle approached the intersection, I saw its brake lights illuminate. The vehicle left the roadway and went airborne. The front end of the vehicle impacted the berm of the interstate hard enough to make the rear raise in the air, then fall back to the ground. I radioed dispatch "He 10-50'd hard into the berm!"

We parked our vehicle in a wide diamond and ordered the driver out of the vehicle. The lights still flashed and the Sergeant's siren still blared through the sound of passing interstate traffic. The driver stumbled out of the vehicle and laid face down on the wet grass. The sergeant and another officer took the driver into custody and I cleared the rest of the vehicle.

There was a spider web crack in the windshield where it appeared the driver's forehead hit due to the impact of the crash.

This case went to trial. The courtroom was full of police officers during closing arguments. The Prosecutor reviewed all of the facts that had been introduced during the course of the trial. He took it a step further during his closing arguments. The Prosecutor got down on his hands and knees and told the jury, "This is the position the officer was in as the vehicle came directly at him. Who is scared for their life? Who is scared for their life?"

Pin dropping would have been audible to anyone in the room. The suspect was convicted and sentenced at a later date.

It was a terrible call to hear on the radio and a dangerous pursuit that followed. We are lucky that no one died.

The Beginning of the End

A former colleague of mine reminded me of an incident that he and I got involved in one early morning. Like most young officers, I was aggressive. I liked to kick butt and take names. We sorted out all of the paperwork afterwards. Always on the hunt for potential crime, sometimes that crime would find me.

I was working the night shift south of the downtown area. 25th Street is a main artery that runs north and south in just about the center of the city. Airplanes landing at the airport line up on 25th Street prior to landing at the airport. At the time, it was four lanes wide making it very easy to turn around on speeders.

The sun hand come up and 25th Street was busy with people driving to get to work. I was headed back to the station for shift change but figured I may be able to pick off a speeder prior to the end of shift. The radar tone is a steady squelch of cars traveling just above and below the posted speed limit. I was about to turn my radar off when it went from the familiar squelch to a high pitched scream. I had never heard a radar tone so high.

Like an alarm clock on steroids waking up a teenager, I initially thought that it may have picked up a landing aircraft. That is when I saw a dark sedan headed towards me. It was weaving wildly in and out of the moving traffic. I hit the lock button on the target, somewhere in the 89 miles per hour range. That is fast in a city. Normally, we would only see motorcycles trying to lose us travel at those dangerous speeds.

By the time I was able to turn around on the dark sedan, it was nearly three blocks ahead of me. Trying to speak over my siren, I called to dispatched and other units that the sedan was traveling at dangerous speeds, endangering everyone on the road. The radio came alive with other units headed my way. One officer said that vehicle matched the description of stolen vehicle from and earlier pre-shift briefing.

The sergeant kept trying to get on the radio to "cancel the pursuit". I thought "what pursuit, I just turned around and haven't even got to 30 miles per hour yet." As the dark sedan approached the busiest crossing avenue, it crashed lighting into another vehicle, then a light pole. The sedan backed up and sped down the busy avenue, turning into an apartment complex.

Another officer and I found the vehicle and ran the plate. Ironically, it can back to someone that lived in the apartment complex. We knocked on the door and spoke with a woman who said her son just got home. She said that he was supposed to be home hours ago, and just showed up now. Because this young man was fearful of his mother's wrath, and ultimately his probation officer's oversight, he endangered the lives of everyone on the road. Well, case solved and now I will charge him out. Unfortunately, this was just the beginning. It would be another lesson in trying to do the right thing, yet have it be wrong.

When I arrived back at the station, I was met with high fives and pats on the back. I was flying high from the excitement. One person who did not feel obligated to congratulate me, us, on a successful collar was the sergeant. He had already grabbed the recording of the radio traffic and was furious. He felt we disobeyed his order to cancel the pursuit, or chase. A chase that really never occurred. He was livid that he could not get on the radio due to all of the other officer's radio traffic. Somehow that was also my fault.

What transpired was me going into private interview rooms, almost daily, to review department policy and dispatch recordings. The same sergeant had some mathematical formula that was just not adding up to make his theory of the incident work. I told him I was driving no more than 30 miles per hour throughout the incident. That statement did not hold water for him, but numbers don't lie. Every day before and after my shift we would go through the same thing, yet nothing ever changed.

I will give him this, the audio recording sounded bad. As I spoke on the radio, you could not only hear my siren, but my tires squealing on the early morning pavement. It is funny now, but it sure didn't not help my case at all. What happened was I used my lights and siren to turn around. They remained on through the first radio transmission, then were turned off. He didn't buy it, and it was starting to piss me off.

After what seemed to be the fifteenth session with this sergeant, I told him, "I have had enough of this shit, do what you have to do!" The problem he had was his elaborate formula, to include the times logged by the dispatcher, were spot on to what I had consistently reported. He took an administrative swing at me and missed. Where he did connect with me was questioning my integrity. He did everything in his power to try and discredit what actually happened, but it didn't add up. What he also did was reinforce the way I was seeing how things worked at certain managerial levels and I wanted no part of it. I see now that this was the beginning of the end for me at this department. It put a terrible taste in my mouth that lingered, no matter how many times I tried to spit it out.

Taking Unnecessary Risks

Sorry to all of my former co-workers. I took some unnecessary risks and made some tactical decisions that in hindsight, were just plain irresponsible and stupid. No one ever got hurt from these decisions made from sheer bravado, but they were still bad.

After the series of stressful incidents while at work, I found myself like an alligator in a murky pond waiting for prey. Give me the good calls, not the stolen bikes and broken windows. I want fast paced, high stress, and violence. My non-professional term for this is "Tackleberry Syndrome". Cadet, and eventually officer, Tackleberry was the over aggressive police officer in the movie Police Academy. Although a comedy, there are several Tackleberry types out there. I had turned into one of them. I mean, that is what it's all about right?

Excitement, danger, and being able to tell unbelievable stories. This could not be more wrong.

Fargo has several trailer parks scattered throughout the city. These trailer parks were like mini cities within the city. I was working the college area, which is a city in itself, when an officer called for assistance regarding an uncooperative individual in one of the north side trailer parks. The initial call was someone allegedly breaking into cars in the trailer park. Now this is what I was talking about.

When I arrived, the officer was situated between her open car door and the body of her squad car. With her firearm out, she had her spot light illuminating an individual in a dark coat. The individual was a mere silhouette, unidentifiable due to the hood and the large coat. The suspect had their head down and hands in their pockets. I pulled up long side the other officer and assumed the same position.

The female officer was ordering the person to show her their hands. The suspect stood like a dark statue and did not comply. The attempt for compliance went on for several minutes and I had enough. It was time to put on my cape and do amazing cop things. This is where my stupidity kicked in.

I didn't tell the female officer what I was about to do which was dumb thing number one. Dumb thing number two is that I actually did it. Like a good soldier in time tested battle tradition, I snuck from my car, around a trailer house, and flanked the suspect. I had a clear line of site at the suspect as I was approximately 25 feet over their left shoulder. I am sure the female officer was wondering where the hell I went.

The suspect, hands still in their pockets, had turned their hooded head in the opposite direction of my hiding spot. This was the perfect time. Like a rock shot from a sling shot, I launched towards them. It was another perfect form tackle. The suspect did not resist. The female officer handcuffed them, conducted a search of their person, and placed them in the rear of her squad car.

She didn't say anything to me. She didn't need to. What she did give me was a look. I will never forget that look. Similar to the look a mother gives a child. A non-verbal scolding that hurts worse than a father's spanking. We never spoke about that call.

After thinking about it, she had her gun pointed right at me. It wasn't her fault, it was mine. One false move by that suspect could have caused a shot to be fired. I could have easily been the recipient of the shot. This was a time when I thought I was ten feet tall and bullet proof. In a moment of clarity, I thought of her having to deal with that type of tragedy and it shook me. What the hell was I thinking. The answer was clear, I was not thinking, I was reacting. My actions during this particular call involved poor judgement and just plain stupidity.

It was the wrong thing to do then, and even more embarrassing to talk about now.

<u>Collateral Duties</u>

With many jobs you may see a small section in the description that says something like, "other duties as assigned". Some of my other duties included Police Explorer Leader and Firearms Instructor, and S.W.A.T. Firearms Range Safety Officer. Collateral duties change with budgets. When our training budget received an increase, so did our firearms training. I loved the S.W.A.T. training. This group of individuals were truly brothers. They trained together, laughed together, and fought with each other just like siblings. When it came to getting a job done, all differences were set aside. They were a well-oiled machine. My job was the Range Safety Officer and Firearms Instructor. I was also the Range Safety Officer for the Sniper Teams. By far, the sniper teams suited me best. I had some training in that arena regarding range estimation ability with the Remington .308.

We did annual S.W.A.T. training at a military base some distance from the metro area. Marksmanship, automatic weapon fire, urban and rural tactics were just a few items covered during this training. I was usually the bad guy in scenarios. It allowed me to observe tactics and provide feedback from what I was able to see during each scenario. Like in the police academy, scenarios can be difficult, but winnable.

The training venue had several different buildings. To practice some of the techniques as a team, a large three level building that resembled a home was the venue. I knew this building well as I had trained there numerous times. There were no windows and plenty of porcupine poop all over the floor.

In the first scenario, I was to simply to hide in a closet. If you have never had an opportunity to be a bad guy for a scenario involving a S.W.A.T. team, it is quite a sight. Other police officers typically make the worst role players because they try way too hard and employ strategy that isn't likely to be encountered on a regular basis. My role was simple, hide in a closet and be compliant when encountered. I was also told not to come out right away.

So I sat down in my closet and waited. There was always a great deal of waiting when you are the bad guy. I heard the thump of boots on the wood floor. The sound methodically moved across the floor below me with voices just over a whisper. The movement would stop, then go again while tiny voices were quietly speaking back and forth.

I could estimate where the group was based simply on the time I had been sitting there. I had been through these scenarios so many times that it made what was happening, very predictable. It is important that people that are role players do exactly what is asked of them.

Apparently one of the role players on the first floor decided to do some impromptu scenario editing on the fly. This changed the way officers interacted with the role players. The cost for that was a set of handcuffs and a close up of the porcupine poop. Unfortunately for me, because of this rogue role player's actions, the S.W.A.T. team decided to up the level of intensity. That is never good for role player number two. As the sound of boots came closer, I made it clear to the team that there was someone inside the closet. I figured if I showed my cooperation, I may get some leniency. A familiar sound clanked on the floor and something that sounded like a bowling ball on a wooden surface came rolling my direction. The floors of this structure are not level. As a matter of fact, they slant towards the closet. Rolling into the quiet, dark closet with me was a flash bang.

We are all about safety, but sometimes things just happen. Unfortunately, these things often happen to me. Some situations are just uncontrollable. Without warning, my vision and hearing were gone. The light pierced my eyes just like a camera flash. The explosion took my hearing and my balance. Before I knew anything else, I was on the floor in handcuffs. At least I was not able to see the porcupine poop on the floor. I needed to have a serious discussion with that first role player.

After recovering from the aftermath of a point-blank flash bang, I discussed sticking to scenario scripts. I volunteered to be a hostage for the next scenario. This would be a low-key role where I would provide complete cooperation. I was a victim in this scenario and was hoping to be treated as such.

Seated on an uncomfortable chair in the middle of an open room, my head was covered with a blanket. This blanket smelled like it had been between a cowboy and horse for eight long, hot, and dusty hours.

I am not sure the S.W.A.T. team had the right intel on this scenario. I heard them come through the door. There was that same metallic clank hitting the uneven floor. Apparently in this room, the floors slanted to the center. The metallic object rolled across the floor and basically right under my wooden chair. All I could do at this point was to let out an audible sigh. When the flash bang erupted, it sent my smelly blanket flying off of my head. I fell backwards onto the floor.

"Someone really needs to clean up all crap on the floor," I thought.

When you start a scenario, it can be stopped at any time for safety reasons. Once everyone knew I was not injured, the hysterical laughter began. I would be hunting this flash bang guy down at some point. I had enough scenarios for one day.

We stayed in the barracks during these training days. They were not fancy rooms, but comfortable enough. The last night there was beer. It was a perfect opportunity to play some pranks on colleagues. One of the team leaders had his room door locked, but his ground floor window was wide open. A couple of us were able to climb into his room and remove every bit of furniture out of his window and reassemble the likeness of his room outside on the lawn. For that, we were chased down and baptized in the cheapest beer available. That night, I was handed my S.W.A.T. shirt and accepted into their brotherhood. It is nice when you have a place to belong.

<u>Getting Hitched</u>

I am not the type of person that follows old traditions. The respect and understandings are there, but the concept does not fit me well. I told my friends I would never date a woman with a child. Never say never. I fell hard for a single mother. She was working three jobs to make it work out for her son. She and her son lived about two miles from me. She had long blond hair all the way to the small of her back. Wearing bib overalls and Converse All-Star shoes, I could tell by her fashion sense we would get along just fine. When she spoke, it was without a filter.

The first time I visited her and Jackson, her son, I came bearing gifts. A hockey stick and other fun gear. He was very excited. We practiced his slap shot right in their living room. Kids that are three or so do not have the best aim or coordination. Jackson seemed to love hockey. As he went to drive the puck into the little net, he missed and struck me directly in the groin. I thought death was at my doorstep.

"Great shot!" I exclaimed, and he kept on swinging. He was a good boy, full of life, and energy. Oh yes, his mom was pretty nice too.

One morning, waiting for her to be done with her shift, I could barely keep my eyes open as something came across the news. It was some awful shooting at a school in Colorado. The name of the school was so unique, Columbine. I watched law enforcement, paramedics, and students running with their hands in the air. I could not fathom the tragedy they were experiencing as they made their way through that school.

I called my future wife and she had been watching the same horror on television. Ironically, 10 years later, one of those deputies that was racing across my old television screen became one of my closest friends. We ended up at the same place in the world, at the same time.

There was no traditional proposal, nor would there be a traditional wedding. Las Vegas seemed the appropriate place for us to wed. We arranged the dates of our travel around the weekend. This was going to be a short turn around. We were married in January 2000. We waited until the middle of the month just in case the infamous Y2K bug would cause disasters throughout the world.

Getting married in Las Vegas really was an amazing experience. We needed a witness to sign our certificate. The only person readily available was Sonny, our limousine driver. Sonny explained that it was certainly not his first signature on a wedding certificate. What tradition did follow was that of returning to the hotel to seal this sacrament.

Hoots, claps and applause met us as we made our way through the lobby and gambling floor of our hotel. The anticipation of what was to come was building. We made it to our floor and down the long haul to our room. Cleaning staff was milling about. I noticed a heavy smell of burning marijuana permeating throughout the entire floor. I didn't care and popped open our door. There is no need to close your eyes for what was to happen next. As we began, our door flew open. A cleaning woman wearing earphones came backing into our room with her cart of cleaning supplies. My very exposed new wife and I stared intently at the cleaning woman, much like we did at the confusing end of the "Blair Witch Project" movie. Mouths open and eyes fixed on the cleaning lady, I really didn't know what to say.

The cleaning woman turned and saw us. I expected her to let out a scream, or give an apology. Instead, she gave a head nod, pulled out her duster, and began dusting the dresser and television area. My wife and I caught each other's expression and absolutely lost it. We laughed. The cleaning woman looked at us and laughed! I am laughing right now. I knew there was something special about this woman, so I married her. If this was happening right after our vows, I could not imagine the rollercoaster she and I were about to endeavor.

When we returned home, it was decided that we would arrange our schedules so that Jackson did not have to attend daycare any longer. My wife would go to work the second I got home from my midnight shift. I would stay up until she was done with her shift, and then I would go to bed. We really didn't have much, but those times were the best. We just made it work.

After a long discussion with my wife, I applied for and was awarded a position in the Narcotics Bureau, adding another piece to the job resume. I could now claim I can shoot, buy and sell drugs, and write standardized reports. A rather limiting skill set for those who seek alternative employment.

Narcs was the best time I had at the police department. The hours varied and the work was challenging. The position was a whole different way of policing. I wore shorts, had grown my hair long, and put all the earrings I once had acquired, back into their respective holes. I looked young, probably because I was young. I did not look like the fella you wanted your daughter to bring home. I drove an undercover car that smelled like cigarettes and Crayola crayons. It puffed blue smoke when starting and accelerating. This little car, known as the blunt, was a very effective undercover unit.

Jackson was starting kindergarten. This would be a first for him, and a first for me. His grandparents and mom would be present for his first day. I also took some time and ran down there. Also present was his biological father. When I walked into the hallway, I received a lot of stares from well-dressed parents. Little did they need to know who I was or what I did for a living. I am certain the most unimpressed was my wife's ex-husband.

Months went by of sharing Jackson with his biological father. The inevitable little jabs and digs were here and there. At one point, we'd all had enough. It was decided to take a different approach to this process. It took a lot of time. It took setting aside differences, egos, and perceptions. It was hard, but ultimately, we all had the same goal. The one thing we could all agree on was that little boy was all that mattered. A truce became effective immediately and permanently.

When I tell people that Jackson's dad comes to everyone's birthdays, every family event, holiday, and maybe just for the occasional happy hour, they pretend to understand. Traditionally all of us are supposed to hold grudges and animosity towards those of whom we have been married or dated. When you enter into reality of what is best for a child, none of the menial and petty things matter. There will always be some sort of connection between all of us through Jackson. We all accepted that and get along. It doesn't always work out that way for others, so we are pretty fortunate. Years later, Jackson's dad admitted that the day he first met me outside Jackson's kindergarten room, he was less than impressed based on my appearance. I take that as a compliment as he had no idea at the time what I did for a living. It is exactly those perceptions and words that we all had to eat, put away, forgive, and move forward from so a little boy could have more dads and grandparents than most children ever get. I guess we all win in the end.

I Knew She was a Keeper

Innovative, creative, assertive, with flashes of brilliance, that describes my wife. Sometimes a little too trusting, and a real sucker for animals, she is always looking to better our lives. Sometimes bettering our lives involves lifestyle changes to better our health. This includes, more sleep, better eating and the occasional fad diet. She has a way of talking me into this by fluttering her eyes and maybe not telling me the entire story of what I am about to agree to do. If this sounds familiar, I am happy that I am not alone.

"I registered us for a class on weight management" she blurted out over dinner one night. "No way," I quickly responded.

I was informed that the registration had been filled out and submitted on my behalf. I am fairly certain that is a felony in some states. Here we go again, another stupid weight loss, get rich quick, work from home licking letters scheme that will be a complete waste of time.

"Whatever," I said, and put it out of my mind.

About a week later, she reminded me that we had our seminar that evening. I tried to think of every excuse in the book to not be available, but could see that me attending this with her was important.

"It will be an adventure," she said.

We piled into the car and headed to one of the local hotels that hosts large conferences. To my surprise there were several people there, more than one hundred. I looked at the registration table and let out a huge sigh of dissatisfaction.

"No way in hell," I said to her.

"Come on, we are already here."

"Weight loss hypnosis Angie, come on!" I responded.

I can not believe the things she has the ability to get me to do. We took our seats and waited for the show to start. I looked around the room and saw all of the other husbands that had the same confused look upon their faces. I can only describe the look as a similar expression of an airline passenger sitting closest to a well-used airplane bathroom. "How did we get here?" seemed to be the non- verbal communication throughout the room.

The hypnotist gave a brief history of the benefits of hypnosis and how he alone could manipulate our minds into not being hungry. All this talk about food though, well, it was making me hungry. I was starting to become impatient when my wife shot me a sharp look. Like a boy who didn't get his sucker at the candy store, I sat with my bottom lip out waiting for this torture to be over.

"I will now hypnotize the entire audience. When you see how this works, you can buy the entire program!" the hypnotists exclaimed.

This strange, deep bass music began to play. To me it sounded like flatulence. Maybe it was flatulence coming from the guy who was snoring in perfect rhythm to the low hum of the bass.

"Think of cool, crisp, lettuce," the hypnotist commanded. I hate lettuce.

I felt pressure in the pit of my stomach. Without warning a growl emerged from my insides like an angry mama bear protecting her cubs. All this talk of food was making me so hungry I could hardly stand it.

When the session was finally over Angie and I looked at each other and began to giggle uncontrollably.

"I am so hungry right now", she exclaimed.

Needless to say, we made a short detour on our way home. Thank God that the Denny's Restaurant is open 24 hours because the "everything omelet" had never tasted so good.

Times Change Things

As my career seemingly moved forward, I found my view on things changing. I slept very little. My patience had become paper thin. I would snap back with sharp words at the smallest of things. I was pretty much angry all of the time. I figured that I was just becoming an old crab. "I have no patience for fools" I would announce more often than not. The smallest of situations could set me off into an angry tirade that could easily last a day or two. I lived in a glass house inside of a glass house. I felt co-workers and family expected me to act or respond a certain way. I had to always rise to the top, because that is where I strived to be. Even the act of my son watching me mow the lawn would cause worried thoughts of a rock hitting him. I was adamant that danger lurked around every corner.

I guess I was a good actor. I could turn on the charm when needed. In reality, I was tired, had headaches constantly, and was always frustrated. These emotions gave me a great deal of energy in the form of anger. Life was exhausting but it was my normal. I was too blind and ignorant to know that if you try and live your life at the top every second of the day, there is only one way to go, and that is down.

Resentment

The old adage that love of money is the root of all evil applies in life's many scenarios. My current neighbors won over 1 million dollars. They had "friends" contacting them they had not heard from in years wishing them well. Along with the well wishes, came sob stories and financial requests. As angelic hearted as they both are, they finally saw the true meaning of these long-lost friends.

Similarly, with a new person in charge of the Police Department, it became evident very quickly who was looking to move up a ladder. Officers, supervisors, all jockeying for position to get ahead. The price they had to pay was swallowing their pride of what they professed prior to the opportunity. Seemingly good people were willing to sacrifice anything and anyone for that one extra stripe or bar on their sleeve. I don't believe patrol had ever seen so many letters of counseling handed out to officers who were just trying to do their jobs. The environment changed to something I had never seen before. It was a divide and conquer, us against them mentality, between patrol and the command staff. The ass kissers were out in full force and had just stocked up on chap stick. I steered clear of all the commotion. This was no longer a place many cared to work.

I realized that I hated this work place. I wanted out. This feeling didn't happen overnight, but I hated it. Working Narcs was the best-case scenario because I did not have to deal with the regular politics. I remember feeling this way just before I got selected for the Narc position. It was about -40 below zero and I was on the night shift. There was absolutely nothing happening so far that night. I came to a four way stop in the center of the city. The other three cars at the four-way stop were police cars. I'd had enough and decided to start looking for something new.

Long after my wife and son went to bed, I was on our dial up internet, job hunting. Every single night I was looking for a different career. I found the perfect position, but a candidate had to be a current federal employee. I had no idea how to do that. The job was for a Firearms Instructor at the Federal Law Enforcement Training Center (FLETC) in Georgia. There was no way my wife would move. There was no way I could take little

Jackson from his friends, grandparents, or biological father. I would sit and wait, and hope something would come along.

I Married a Vampire

When I was working Narcs, my wife worked at the local hospital. She would get up at about 3 am and drive around the city to different nursing homes, drawing blood from patients. I had married a vampire.

My wife drove a Mustang convertible. It was about 4:30 a.m. one morning when my phone rang. My wife was frantic on the other end of the line. She told me that she was scared for her life. A car had been following her while she was collecting her blood draws. As she sped up to get away, the vehicle began to chase her. She headed for the well-lit hospital canopy area where, like a cop's wife's reasoning, there would be security cameras.

"I don't know if I will be able to make it through the security door before this car will be right on top of me" she said. I told her to head to fifth street and make her Mustang fly southbound towards our house. I could hear the fear in her voice and it pissed me off. "Come to me," I said.

It was a pitch black, the darkest part of the night. She could not give a description of the vehicle that was chasing her. There wasn't much going to be moving around the city this time of night. It would be easy for me to pick out both vehicles. I loaded my stainless-steel Marine Magnum shotgun with three rounds of slugs and one 00 buck shot for good measure.

The slugs are heavy chunks of lead with a rounded nose that can cause devastation to whatever they encounter. That would include vehicles chasing my wife. The 00 buck shot contained nine .32 caliber balls that flew through the air and are able to cover a larger area. On my thigh, was my Glock .40 with several rounds of ammunition. I would not likely be needing any handcuffs.

I threw on my vest that read in large bold letters "POLICE". Like a marshal in a cowboy town, I stood ready, waiting for two sets of headlights. On the boulevard in front of our house was a large oak tree. Heavily armed and with Mother Nature's cover and concealment, I would have a definite advantage.

"Stay on the phone with me and floor it" I ordered. "Drive past the tree, park by the sidewalk, go inside, I will be right there". I heard the roar of a mustang rapidly approaching our quiet neighborhood. As the sound drew closer, a set of familiar headlights quickly turned towards me, just as instructed. And now I waited. She did just as I said.

I leveled the shotgun down the empty avenue and waited. I thought about how this may go down. I was pissed, and a lesson was about to be taught.

Nothing came through, down, or by our avenue. There was no sound, no lights, nothing. Whoever had been chasing my wife lacked her driving skills and the power of a 302 engine in a Mustang GT. She clearly out ran and maneuvered the vehicle that was terrorizing her. I had never heard or seen her so scared in my life. This was unacceptable to me. No one does this to one of my tribe. This situation only made me angrier and more distrustful of the world. For me to be a cop and a victim was embarrassing and unacceptable. If I ever found out who this was, they would pay dearly.

Let's Get Physical

In law enforcement, we are often tested to our limits both mentally and physically. My collateral duty included representing the department as a firearms instructor. It was a good fit considering my job as a weapons instructor with the Air National Guard. I also enjoyed my time with shooters that struggled with firearms.

There are certain inherent dangers one faces as a firearms instructor. At the end of a day at the range, I would be mentally exhausted. Constant vigilance, on the lookout for safety, and providing instruction to many people who didn't want to be there, can be difficult. Safety violations often times went in waves.

The department required officers to take periodic physicals. These were completed at the public health building across the street from the department. Firearms instructors were given blood tests to determine if there were unsafe levels of lead within their blood. I had this done several times prior and was not at all concerned when I found my notice to take a physical in my department mail box. I noticed that this would be a full physical, including a hernia check. If you don't know, that often requires a physician to examine the testicular area of a male, having the patient turn their head and cough. This was no different than a high school sports physical.

I made my way across the street and sat in the waiting room with the rest of the patients waiting to see one of many public health doctors. The waiting room was completely full. I walked around until I found a seat. After about 30 minutes, my name was called and I proceeded into one of the exam rooms that opened directly into the crowded waiting room.

I always wondered what those little colored things outside the exam room door frame were for. I could only assume they were to indicate what portion of care the patient may be receiving at the time. As I entered the room, I noticed that none of my color things were in use. The nurse proceeded to take my blood pressure, other vital signs, and drew a vial of blood. She told me that the doctor would be in shortly to finish the exam.

After about 30 more minutes, a doctor entered the room and asked me some medical questions. I answered as I always have. So far, this had been a rather unremarkable doctor visit.

"Stand up. Drop your pants. We are going to check for a hernia" the doctor ordered

I complied and turned my head to the left, preparing to cough. The doctor took a knee and grabbed what he needed to grab to complete the test. Just as he made contact, the door of the exam room flew open, exposing me to an even more crowded waiting room. I felt like a light bulb that a doctor was changing. The loud waiting room grew silent as a church during a funeral. I am rarely speechless, but at that point, I had nothing. The nurse turned to see what everyone in the waiting room was staring at.

"Oh my god, I am so sorry!" The nurse exclaimed.

She quickly left, slamming the door behind her.

"Wow, ummm, you're good," the doctor announced.

The worst part was having to leave the examination room. I didn't know if I would be met with laughter, whispers, or applause. I put my hat down as far as it would go and made my way directly to the exit. I can tell you this, that was my one and only time of public exhibitionism.

<u>Prosthetics</u>

Practical jokes are a huge part of law enforcement. The best ones are both practical and jokes. There are definite advantages to working the night shift. No management to deal with, interesting calls, and aggressive officers making a difference.

October seems to be a natural time of year for pranks. On one particular night, an officer had been dispatched to a call in a quiet residential neighborhood. Someone had put a pair of fake legs under a vehicle. Later in the shift, the legs made their appearance in the locker room. Those kinds of things.

My locker was located by one of the many bathrooms. The bathrooms all contained a sink, stool, and shower. As I changed after my shift, the detectives would already have arrived for the day shift. One detective in particular had this strange obsession with taking his morning constitution in the bathroom right by my locker. When he was finished, the smell punished anyone who was even within 30 feet. I don't know what this detective had in his daily diet, but it most certainly included eggs. That seemed to cause others to think that this bathroom was something special. I have no idea why that particular room was so popular, but something needed to be done about this situation.

It didn't matter if one of the other six bathrooms was available, like a homing pigeon, this detective and others always came back to the bathroom by my locker. Day after day we would be greeted with this torture. I'd had enough. I went on the search for the fake legs.

I found the legs in an empty locker. They were already wearing pants and shoes. This was going to be perfect. With the help of friends, I placed the prosthetic legs in the stall. Steve was the smallest, so he locked the door on the inside and crawled under the divider. We turned the light on and shut the door. Now it was just a matter of time to see if this was going to have the effect we hoped it would have.

Person after person opened the door and apologized to the legs. The presentation was impeccable. The stench had stopped for now. One of the night shift supervisors had taken a liking to that bathroom as well. He plowed through the door only to see the legs on the stall. "Oh jeez, sorry" he exclaimed. I could not help but letting out a little yelp of laughter. The next night was the same situation. The same supervisor opened the door only to be greeted with the same pair of legs, followed by another apology. This was great.

The third night, the same supervisor walked into the bathroom. I did everything I could to not start laughing. He entered the bathroom and stopped. He held the door open with his foot and stared silently at the stall.

"Hey buddy, are you okay in there?" he called out to the legs. Turning around he had a look of concern on his face. I had a tear that had welled up in my eyes from trying to contain my laughter.

"Hey, are you okay?" he yelled again. I am laughing at this point. He walked to the stall and tried to open the door which was still locked.

Louder now he called "Hey, are you okay in there?" The supervisor grabbed his shoulder microphone and started calling dispatch. We were ready for this and used a technique called "covering" on his radio transmission. This is done by multiple people keying their radios causing his radio transmission to be inaudible.

He was a high-strung guy and we had to end this prank before he kicked the stall in. After explaining to the supervisor what he had been negotiating with, he showed a great appreciation for the ingenuity. We got the stall door open and removed the legs. They would show up at another prank to be determined in the future. The supervisor laughed, shut the door, and we were back where we started.

<u>**Movies, Food, and Bad Drivers**</u>

When you live in the cold northland, the days are short and the nights are long. Darkness falls about 4:30 p.m. and you will not see daylight until about 7:00 a.m. the next day. The cold winter months limit what there is to do for recreation. A common recreational theme up north is going out to eat. It doesn't matter what night of the week, call ahead seating is always recommended.

On a cold November evening, my wife and I had just finished what we call "supper" at a local restaurant. The snow had not yet touched the ground. It was about 7:30 p.m. and we were headed home. It was Friday, and for shift work, it was actually my Sunday. We were traveling down our usual route that led almost directly to our house. The radio was blaring some sort of metal music, likely Metallica.

Driving my wife's Mustang, we cruised through the downtown area. It is interesting to see people bar hopping this time of year. Typically, people 40 years and older are bundled up in hat and long coats. College kids, because it's not cool to be warm, wear t-shirts and short skirts. Although it was cold out, the night could not have been more beautiful. There was no wind, and a bright moon shined down upon the city. There was a full moon. I don't know if there is any truth to the full moon causing people to act out or not.

From traffic light to traffic light I watched. People yelling, some singing, others darting across the street in front of moving cars. A disturbing feeling started down low in my gut. That feeling that something was just off. It is that feeling, almost like Deja vu, where you feel like you are living a moment all over again. I didn't know what that moment was, but I was certain that something was likely to happen. I kept this feeling to myself and decided to find the most direct route out of the downtown area.

When we cleared the downtown area, I thought the feeling would subside. Instead of me relaxing, knowing we were less than a mile from home, I became more alert than ever. I was focused on a vehicle that had been behind us for some time. I had noticed how the vehicle would accelerate rapidly and brake very close to us at every single light. Approaching the final light before we reached home, the vehicle sped at us and slid to a stop, nearly hitting our rear bumper. I'd had enough at this point.

While waiting at the red light, I called dispatch from my cell phone. I described the situation, location, and a vehicle description the best I could. What I did next was probably not the best idea, but after my wife's encounter with someone chasing her, I handed my cell phone to my wife and told her to stay on the line with dispatch. With badge in hand and an off duty weapon on my hip, I got out and approached the vehicle that was behind us.

I yelled "Police" and told the driver to shut the vehicle off. The driver did not comply. "Turn the vehicle off now!" I ordered. The driver looked wide eyed at me. He threw the car in reverse and spun remnants of gravel towards me. The vehicle then turned left, nearly striking me, maneuvering around our Mustang. I hopped in my car and began to follow them.

The vehicle made a series of erratic turns, and headed down several residential streets. There was not much traffic so it was easy to see where the car was. The vehicle cut through a church parking lot, and back on to a residential street. I was a good two blocks behind them when they shut their lights off. I was relaying locations to dispatch. When they shut their lights off, the game changed a little. Behind me I could see the cavalry. The red, white, and blue emergency lights pierced the darkness as they sped past us.

The squads chased the darkened car for about three more minutes. The driver, and passenger had attempted to jump out of the vehicle and enter a residence. They were confronted by the police in the entry way of a small house that had been converted to apartments. They both denied being in the vehicle, even though the driver had the keys in his possession. The driver was cited for multiple violations and released. I provided a detailed statement for the responding officers.

The interesting thing about these situations are a person would think they are clear cut. I have learned that there is no such thing as clear cut. The driver decided that going to court was his best option. After providing a very unconvincing "I was scared" defense, the driver was convicted of every citation. That was followed up by a scolding from the judge.

Was it right or wrong of me to get out of my vehicle and confront this driver? In hindsight, probably not. I look back and ask myself why I did that. Was it the result of a compound list of things transpired in the months earlier? Clearly it was an unnecessary risk that I could have handled differently. Presently, I would use much more brain power than bravado to handle a similar situation.

<u>Who Done It?</u>

In the Bible, the book of Proverbs has a verse that says. "Idle hands are the devil's workshop". This could not be truer with bored law enforcement officers. The joking never tends to cease. It really never matters how much or little time that a law enforcement officer has on a department, they are fair game to any and all practical jokes. To be honest, a shift as a law enforcement officer can go from days of boredom followed by days of intense excitement. Coping with this roller coaster ride of events is often expressed with officers planning elaborate practical jokes to play upon each other.

A young and motivated sergeant is the key to a successful team. Working the night shift, I had just that. My sergeant was not only motivated, but also an advocate for those he supervised. The sergeant was also an easy target for practical jokes. With that being said, he became the victim of many elaborate pranks, but took each in stride. I think he knew that part of leadership was accepting these pranks as signs of the respect we had for him. Interesting things happen in any city when the lights go out, even to sergeants.

On a cool fall Sunday evening, our regular night shift crew started to conspire on our next prank. That evening we had decided to all meet for coffee at a centralized 24-hour restaurant. The restaurant was always police friendly and understanding when we had to leave in the middle of a meal. This particular night shift crew was the best group of men and women I would ever work with while I was a police officer. We respected each other, knew what each would do or say before it was even done or spoken. We were effective in everything we did, including acts of tomfoolery.

The bars had closed about an hour prior to our meeting at the restaurant. When I pulled into the lot, there were already four squad cars backed into spots. In case you didn't know, law enforcement officers have a habit of backing into parking spaces. This is one of the behaviors that follows us even with our personal vehicles. One of the first things I noticed was a bright new, flawless squad car. My sergeant had received his first new squad car in his many years at the police department. He was beaming from ear to ear as he opened the door and exited the cruiser. The odor of a urine and regurgitated Purple Passion that accompanied some squad cars was missed. Instead, that new car smell filled the cool night air.

My sergeant and three other officers went inside the restaurant and sat down. Another squad pulled up with a veteran officer. This woman was an amazing officer. Her calm demeanor was consistent, night after night, regardless of what situation we faced. To this day I consider her the best officer the department ever had.

"Hey, check it out" she said.

"Do I dare ask what's in the bag?" I replied.

She opened the bag and I started to laugh. Like glistening diamonds, there were shards of broken glass. I knew where this was going. Somehow, she also managed to get a key for the sergeant's new squad car. I could see that the sergeant was already seated with the other officers and surely on his third war story by now.

We quietly opened the new squad car door. That new car smell filled my nose again. We rolled the window down all of the way. The officer opened her trunk and produced the metal handle of a broom. We took the broom and placed it through the now open window and rested it on the new squad car seat. With the pillow case in hand, glass was spread on the ground directly below the open window.

"Time to eat!" she exclaimed.

This restaurant had the best cinnamon rolls you could find. Because the bars had closed prior to our visit to the restaurant, there were some louder than average customers filling their beer munchie craving. The loud customers left about fifteen minutes after our arrival. This was playing into our prank perfectly. The anticipation was killing me.

We all paid, and like a good sergeant, he was the last out the door. As he approached his shiny new squad car, he stopped dead in his tracks. Before him was the crime scene. Based on his reaction, you would have thought he was watching a Stephen King horror film. His eyes were wide as he stood there with his mouth wide open. He tried to speak, but all that came out were grunts and a high-pitched whistle. I did everything I could not to laugh.

"Whoa, what happened?" one officer said.

"God damnit, those loud assholes did this!" he insisted.

Ranting and raving about how he was going to finger print everything and process all of the DNA evidence he could. He was scanning the parking lot for video cameras and potential witnesses.

The female officer opened the door of his now damaged squad car.

"Be careful, there is probably glass in there" he told the female officer.

His temper seemed to build like a muscle cramp. The vein in his temple would have caused a phlebotomist to salivate. I do not recall everything he said because most of it was incoherent.

"Hey Sarge" the female officer called.

She moved the metal broom handle out of the seemingly broken window and let it clang to the ground. She hit the window button, and with a slight hum of the window motor, the perfectly clear window rolled up to its original position.

The same look of shock fell across the sergeant's face. At this point, I lost it. I laughed so hard I thought I was going to visit my cinnamon roll a second time. Roars of laughter from the other officers rumbled throughout the parking lot. The Sergeant's look of shock turned into a look of relief when he knew he had been pranked.

I do not recall exactly what the sergeant's words were, but I do know they included calling us certain body parts that are typically located between the knee caps and below the waist line. The best part was I think that he appreciated the time and effort that was put into this prank. The collecting of glass, stealing of a key, a metal broom handle, and distracting him while the entire plan was executed.

I miss this crew because they were truly my family.

One Last Trip to Camp

September was always a magical time for me. It meant college football, cooler weather, and our week of S.W.A.T. training at the local military base. I rode with a fellow officer to the training facility in his personal vehicle. We had known each other for some time. We did not really know any intimate details of each other's lives other than spouses. I knew he and his wife had no children and enjoyed activities such as biking, hiking, and camping.

On this day I could tell something was eating him up inside. He told me that he had just found out that he was a father and that his child was already a teenager. I probably didn't help much as I sat staring at him, mouth wide open, shaking my head back and forth. I guess this could happen to just about anyone. I took a quick inventory of my past and was reasonably certain that I would be in the clear of a situation like that. This trip was starting out in a very different way than usual.

Each training deployment provided me something to experience. My ears and eyes had recovered from our last deployment. I would spend the majority of time with the snipers this week. Snipers, especially those with military training, are truly a unique bunch of professionals. They are passionate, precise, a little weird, clever, perfectionistic, and quite eccentric. Law Enforcement snipers kind of do their own thing. Like different sections of a police department, some specialize in certain aspects of the mission. I fit in perfectly with this crew.

Lying comfortably on a berm about 300 yards from the live fire house, the sniper teams were practicing sniper-initiated assaults. Essentially, the sniper shoots over the heads of the S.W.A.T. members waiting at the door. The shot is typically well above their heads, often times in a second story window. When the S.W.A.T. members hear the report or impact, they begin their task. This drill had been done several times over on this particular day. We began to place different objects in the upstair's window of the live fire house. A teddy bear, cans, used flash bang containers, whatever was available.

There was a slight cross wind on this day. My spotter was not a cop, but instead an Army Ranger. I liked this guy because he was quiet and a phenomenal spotter. Jim, one of the snipers, ran down to hang up a flash bang on a string. I watched through my binoculars as he tied it into the window frame. As he was running half way back it fell to the ground. I waited until he got all the way back to inform him of that, of course.

"Jim, the flash bang fell, can you go hang it back up again?" I said with a smile. Jim trotted the 300 yards back to the second level and restrung the string holding the used flash bang back into the window frame. He sure was out of breath when he got back, but said nothing.

I saw the S.W.A.T. team start to assemble which indicated they were nearly ready to move into position. I looked at my spotter and said, "I am going to shoot that string and Jim will have to go hang it up again."

He never took his eyes off his spotting scope and said, "Ya, that would be hilarious." I had just called a shot that would clearly be very unlikely.

I inched in behind the Leupold scope and found the flash bang dancing in the window frame. The wind swung the flash bang side to side in the window frame. Back and forth it danced. One other attribute that snipers often possess is observance. Patterns, shapes, and other stimulus plow into short term memory and are evaluated at the speed of light. I noticed with the breeze that when the flash bang moved to my left, there was a strange air current that consistently held my target in the position for about two seconds.

The S.W.A.T. team was in position and the scenario was about to begin. I had been observing for five minutes prior to that radio call. "I have the target" I stated.

"Send it!" the spotter responded. The timing was perfect. My sight picture was just as consistent as the last two swings of the flash bang. Before the "t" was out of the spotter's mouth, the trigger on my .308 was already pressed. The loud thump, and slight bump it gave into my shoulder indicated the round was on its way. I watched as the flash bang fell straight to the floor from its suspended position.

"Holy shit!" exclaimed the spotter.

"Jim, it fell again!" I exclaimed.

"You are such a dick" was the response.

I am not professing that I actually shot a string with a .308 from 300 yards on a windy day, but it sure looked that way. Upon further inspection, there was no bullet hole in the flash bang, only a torn string that once held what was supposed to be the target.

There are a lot of things that could have cut that string. Wood from the backstop, shrapnel from the round falling apart. But that day, we could at least believe that it actually happened. I called it. It appeared to have happened. And I felt good about it. I kept the flash bang and broken string as a trophy. Mainly because I am a little weird and eccentric.

My September 11

It was about 7:45 A.M. Central Time. I was watching my 13inch television and could not believe my eyes. Some idiot had crashed a jet into the World Trade Center. This was horrific. I took a quick shower and started putting on my camouflage. It was about 8:00 a.m. and I was ready to head out for the second to the last day of training, when another plane hit the south tower. Obvious to all, this went from a horrific accident to an intentional act of terrorism.

I left the barracks and everyone was talking about the planes hitting the towers. We made our way to the berm and began doing some precision slow fire. It was about 8:45 when the S.W.A.T. commander placed his hand on my right shoulder. It was almost some kind of fatherly gesture. He told me and others of a third attack that had happened minutes earlier. A third civilian aircraft had crashed into the Pentagon. All National Guard personnel were to gather their things and report to their respective guard units immediately.

My eyes were wide, my mind had questions, but I found myself sitting in another officer's vehicle headed back to Fargo. We stopped in a small town to get fuel. Both still in our S.W.A.T. camouflage, people came and patted us on the back.

"Get those sons of bitches!" one man exclaimed. The people in the gas station seemed to support this notion. I did not know it at the time, but that was the last day I would work for the Fargo Police Department.

Part III

The Soldier

I won't say much about my military service, not now. I will tell you that the soldiers I served with were the best. They still are the best. They were like my own little dysfunctional family. We were young and willing to take on the challenges our commanders presented to us. I was fortunate to have great support and leadership during my active duty service.

I traded in one camouflage uniform for another. I was now wearing the uniform that I typically used one weekend a month and two weeks a year. Quickly placed on Title 10 orders, which means active duty, the next month or so would reveal how long this situation was going to last. Normally, the National Guard is deployed for short duration. Natural disasters, detail deployments, and annual training are what a Guardsman is used to being subjected. After the first month, I started wondering if maybe the second month would bring an end to the active duty orders. I started on the day shift, reviewing current security plans and preparing for weapon qualifications.

Three months passed. I started to wonder if there was a much larger picture than I could see. I missed being a Narc, but I had been a guardsman a lot longer. Out of nowhere, they divided us into squads. I was assigned as one of the Noncommissioned officers (NCO) to Squad 2. I was one of three Fargo Police Officers that had been activated and served with Squad 2. Our job was base security, working the night shift. It was now December and there was no end in sight of my active duty service.

I had fallen into a very comfortable role with Squad 2. My enlistment date had come and gone. It was the beginning of the Global War on Terror, and we were all staying until further notice.

December turned into January, and that is when the call came. Squad 2 was being deployed to a "Classified Location". A DD214 is a record of military service. My DD214 still says "Classified Location" today. This causes problems sometimes at the VA. I had never heard of the country to which I was being deployed, but the map indicated it was right in the middle of the most reported area in the world at the time. When February rolled in, we rolled out.

The alarm woke my wife and me about 4:00 a.m. on the morning of my departure. Our son slept with us that previous night. I didn't wake him, I just couldn't. He knew I was leaving, but we really didn't provide him with the details. It was the first time I was leaving my family since we met and it hurt like hell. It was also the first time I looked deep into my wife's eyes. She didn't say much. She didn't need to. I saw hurt, fear, sadness, and pride. We found it best to not say anything at all, hugged, and I left.

I rode with one of the other soldiers and his mother to the Fixed Base Operator (FBO) where a Navy 727 awaited us. As we unloaded from the car, she grabbed me by the arm. "Promise you will look after him," She said. Her eyes were blood shot from the early morning and from silent tears. Those words sound stereotypical, almost out of a movie, but it doesn't feel that way when a mother is speaking about their child.

"I will" is all I could muster. What did I just promise this woman? I knew very little of what was in store for us. I knew I had my chemical gear and a bunch of other gear that I had never used, but that was all.

Atlanta Again

Stop number one was Hartsfield-Jackson International in Atlanta, Georgia. Here we would wait for other units to assemble. Once the assigned units arrived, we would board a large rotator plane and head towards even warmer weather. Bless those folks at the USO for putting up with Squad 2 for twelve hours. During our wait, these folks provided us with food and entertainment. I hadn't realized what an awesome organization the USO was until I experienced what they do first hand.

During this time we honed our card playing skills and rested as the rest of our journey was going to be long. We made out way to the check-in area and boarded our large civilian rotator plane. It was a huge L1011 chartered by a private airline. The flight attendants were very gracious and patient with our testosterone-filled cabin. One in particular agreed to play a joke on a fellow Squad 2 soldier. We kept paging him to the aft of the plane. He wandered around the plane asking people were the aft was located. He is now a commercial pilot.

Germany

Stop number two was in Germany. From my small window, I watched the plane go down, come up, and go down, again.

"Now I can say I have been here" I thought.

They kept us corralled like cattle in a separate area of the airport. We were not allowed to leave and were told that the plane was being replenished. More soldiers arrived and joined us in our make shift pen. It was dark and there were not enough seats in the waiting area. Soldiers laid on the floor waiting for our call to board. After about two hours, we were herded back on to our plane.

If you ever have been on a plane for an extended amount of time then asked to deplane while they perform airplane things, it is kind of like walking into someone else's home. Each home has a different feel and smell. Walking onto a plane where a bunch of hormonal soldiers have been sitting for four hours, well, let's just say that I would have paid $100 for a can of Febreze.

Into the Oven

I have been in hot places, but not like desert hot. When I got off the plane and started making my way across the large flight line, it felt like an oven door had been opened and the oven was left on.

I had brought my lap top computer with me on this journey. I enjoyed taking photos and editing them on my computer. One piece of information that we were told before we left home was not to have any pornography in our possession while we cleared the host country's customs. I was certain that would not be issue for me.

I had a photograph of my wife taped to the top of my computer. It was from a rare trip we had taken with her sister to Aruba. We were still paying on the credit card for that one. It was a beautiful picture. Her long blonde hair was highlighted by the back drop of the blue water. She had a wide smile and was wearing her bikini with matching sarong. I don't know if my wife takes it as a compliment or criticism, but in this part of the world, her beauty was on the same level of highly paid porn actresses such as Stormy Daniels and Jenna Jameson.

The picture of my wife was removed from my laptop cover. I am certain the little bastard took it and went immediately on break, looking for some privacy. I guess this part of the world has a different view of things. Of course, they didn't bother to check the other 3,000 similar pictures on the hard drive of my computer. Boy would they have been in for a shock.

Everything was drab in this new environment, mainly tan in color. The gray color of military aircraft was the only subtle contrast. Our tent was amazing. A small rat-like creature scurried away as I opened the door. The tent had a wooden floor and a wooden door. It was surprisingly much better than I expected. Simply getting out of the sun was quite a relief on my pale North Dakota skin tone.

The distant hum of generators would seem to be an annoyance. There was a box at the rear of the tent that resembled a central air conditioning unit. This unit hummed in tune with other distant generators. I could feel warm air moving slightly throughout the tent. It smelled stale.

Inside the tent was a wide open space. There were cots, a set of bunk beds and some make-shift dressers. I chose a cot in the middle. This was now home until further notice.

I started unpacking my gear and noticed something disturbing. Part of our gear included military-issue bug spray and sun screen. My sun screen had leaked out on to my goggles. I used the goggles to protect my eyes while riding in the gun turret of our armored Humvees. The sun screen had eaten entirely through my protective goggles.

"And they want me to put this on my skin?" I thought. I decided that my sleeves would stay down the entire deployment.

The First Job is the Worst Job

I would like to think I am not a dumb man. I mean, I sneaked through college and have some work experience. I rely on common sense as my compass. When I was told what I was going to be doing as my first job in this new world, the title sounded rather harmless. It was the concept with which I took issue. Because I was a weapons instructor, I was qualified on just about every weapon in the inventory. This made sergeants happy because I could be plugged in the roster wherever there was a hole.

"Hudson! Fuel escort," the sergeant announced. I didn't know what that was, but it didn't sound terrible.

I drew my M9 pistol from the armory. I was also given a portable radio. I don't know a whole lot about the technical aspects of portable radios. I do know that since my activation, the radio I had was mainly for show. This radio, unless you were in the line of sight of someone, was really nothing more than something to balance out the weight of my pistol on the opposite side of my hip.

Fuel escorts had a simple job. They escorted fuel trucks. That sounded easy enough to me. When I arrived at the search pit where the fuel trucks were searched prior to heading to their destination, I asked where our vehicle was located. "One should be rolling in shortly" was the response.

A semi-truck pulled into the search pit. Soldiers and dogs began their inspection. There was a cab, sleeper area, and it pulled a tanker trailer. I was told earlier that all fuel to the flight line was being trucked as the pipeline had not yet been constructed. I was still looking for my vehicle. What I didn't realize is that the truck and driver before me *was* my vehicle. This is how fuel escort worked.

I was to get into a vehicle with a stranger, in a country that didn't particularly care for us, and ensure that this driver took a load of jet fuel to the correct location? Keep in mind also that the Department of Transportation in this country did not necessarily have the same stringent guidelines as the United States for hours worked or truck safety. It is not like I could ask the driver for his log book as he probably couldn't have understood me anyway, and I'm pretty sure he didn't have one.

I continued analyzing this new job I had so lovingly acquired. Driving at 50-60 mph, what if the driver decides to go rogue and make his truck a missile, like the planes that hit the World Trade Center? My job was to stop him. I would draw my M9 and prevent this inevitable tragedy. So, now if I did have to shoot the driver, I would find myself riding in a truck at 60 mph, pulling a full load of jet fuel that would be speeding into a sand berm. I would say at this point, I would be in a cruise missile and would be done for. Not to mention the .50 caliber team that had their weapon pointed directly down the road at oncoming traffic. If that gem started firing lead my way, at least my demise would likely be instantaneous.

This job sucked. I rode in about nine trucks that first night. It was awful. I was on edge every second. We had a definite language barrier. The drivers had been working so long they were falling asleep while driving. When we would get in line at the off-load site, they would jump into the sleeper for about five minutes of rest. I was just waiting for one to hop out with a butcher knife.

Should there have been one driver that attempted to go the wrong way towards tent city or directly to the aircraft, we would have both died. He for whatever cause, and me to protect personnel and valuable resources. I have no idea how many rides I took in these trucks, maybe 50 or 100. I never made any friends with the fuel truck drivers. They knew why I was there, I knew why I was sitting with them. We left it at that. I needed to find a different job.

I am not sharing a lot of military stories. Those stories deserve their own private venue. As time went on, I rotated between different posts and never rode in a fuel truck again. Sometimes I was the stationary M60 Machine gun post, or the M60 gunner on an armored Humvee, or on interior law enforcement patrol and even flight line security response personnel. I liked the variety. We had several things happen while on shift. Each incident we treated with the same level of vigilance and with tactics for which we were trained. At the end of our shifts, we would work out. That is what we did, worked, worked out, then tried to sleep.

There was quite a bit of down time. A day off didn't occur very often, but I was perfectly fine with that. The more I worked, the faster this commitment would move. I started to ponder my career. I was stationed with other soldiers from National Guard units all over the United States. We got along best with the New Yorkers and Texans. I think the New Yorkers were amazed that people could live where we did because of the "isolation" and weather. The Texans, well we were pretty much the same folk, just with different accents.

During my interactions with other solders, I learned about Federal Law Enforcement. I learned of the work and pay they received. I learned that I hated my job at the police department. The more I told people I loved it there, the more I despised the thought of ever returning to that job. I never told anyone that, I just quietly started looking for a different career.

Sleeping was nearly impossible in this desert land. During the day, the tent city came alive. It was difficult to sleep because I was working nights and needed to sleep during the day.   The thunder of war planes, the rumble of track vehicles, dozers, and other loud activities took place during the day time hours. Just when there would be a break in the activity, a call to prayer would sound out from a mosque. According to my fellow soldiers, I began to snore loudly and thrash violently in my cot. I would call out in my sleep. I had daily headaches and was short tempered.

"Whatever," I thought. I am on the other side of the world and it smells like a sewer. I get to be a jerk now and then.

As time passed in the desert, I was able to make a few calls home. Care packages were always an exciting time. My family tends to have a very awkward sense of humor. My wife spent about a week packing a large container containing beef jerky, news articles, movies, and perfectly packaged bottles of Listerine mouth wash. It mixed perfectly with Coke Lite. Military personnel love Listerine mouth wash. Heat sealed appropriately, it's color and consistency are nearly identical to Jack Daniel's whiskey. Oral hygiene is important in warm climates.

My father- in -law, as a joke, packed me some old underwear and other worthless items, knowing my wife was sending her package. My wife sent me an email that the package was on its way. I waited, and waited, but nothing came.

One day, I decided to check the mail call. I found a package with my name on it. Excited that I could finally rinse my mouth out, I opened the box. In the box there was a pair of underwear and other items that I had absolutely no use for. A used comb, a small sombrero, and a cassette recorder. This must have been the joke box, so the real deal must not be far behind. If I were to have waited there until it came, I would still be there. The package my wife took so much time and care packing had gone missing.

Heading Home

We would not be flying commercial. We were hopping a ride on a KC 135 refueler from the Grand Forks, ND Air Force Base. Grand Forks was a short hour drive from Fargo. We turned in all of our bedding and other items issued when we had first arrived.

It was exceptionally hot that day. The flight plan was to fly to England, spend the night, and then fly all the way back to Grand Forks AFB. We rode in a deuce and a half truck to our awaiting escape vessel. Inside the plane felt like a pressure cooker. The plane's engines roared, then a loud snap, and then shut off. This happened at least three times.

We were told that leaving that day was not an option. Back to our tents we went. I have to say, I just was not surprised. My luck had seemed to have gone from bad to worse as the days moved on. I had grown to expect these types of things to happen. Luckily, the next day, we were airborne. After some Tylenol PM, I closed my eyes and felt like this may be the first good rest I'd had in a long time.

I was awakened after what seemed like a half hour. The soldier who woke me, told me that we were going to be landing in England shortly. Land we did! When the plane doors opened I could smell the humidity. It had just rained and the grass was so green. The cool wet breeze felt like heaven. We were sent to our private rooms.

My room was impeccable. It had cable and the World Wrestling Federation was on. My son and I loved professional wrestling. I was not sharing space under a canvas cloth with ten other people. I am not a bath guy, but on this day, I made an exception. When the tub drained, I was baffled as to where all of the sand had come from. There are only a few select places that could have been hiding places considering it was a bath. I went to bed, and I slept.

The next day we boarded the KC 135 and we were bound for home. The Tylenol PM thing worked before, and it worked again. When we landed, we had to clear our own customs. They required us to brush our boots and remove any contraband. I don't know to what contraband they were referring, perhaps the case of Cuban Cigars?

I stood there, waiting to get through the line. My wife was on the other side. We just stared at each other. After I was finally cleared, we were reunited and complete again. Well, almost.

"What do you want to do first?" she asked.

"McDonalds, quarter pounder combo, two cheeseburgers!" I exclaimed. We hit the drive through and headed back towards our home. I had to stop at two rest areas after that McDonald's meal. I guess I should have paced myself.

We headed directly to pick up our son from his father's apartment in Fargo. When we pulled up to the curb, there he was! He knew I would be home in the near future, but didn't know which day. My wife kept it a secret. I yelled and started running. After about ten feet, my son stopped dead in his tracks.

"Dan!" he yelled, and plowed into my waiting arms. We headed to our small house and I got out of that nasty desert - colored uniform. We laid on the trampoline in our back yard.

"When did we get a trampoline?" I asked myself.

As we lay there, I told my wife that now I could have some peace and quiet. Just as I said that, four loud Navy FA 18's flew in formation directly over us.

"Great, the Blue Angels are here this weekend for the air show" my wife sighed. We all laughed because that is the way things go for us. The War on Terror separated us for a bit but it didn't matter, because we knew we were finally complete again.

My New Life

My first night home, I had nightmares. I had more and more nightmares that usual. Not the normal type, but very vivid images that seemed as if they were real -- like trailers from a movie preview; terrible, intense, stressful scenes replayed. I did not know what sleep apnea was, but if you take the symptoms out of a medical manual it described my lack of sleep to perfection.

The worst of it came a short time after I came back home. We were at my in-law's lake place when I was awakened by a massive blow to the left side of my head. When my true vision revealed what was happening, I was on top of my wife with both hands around her throat.

She is not one to take something like this lying down. I don't know what she struck me with but judging by the ringing in my left ear, I would guess it to be a nearby telephone. This wasn't right and scared the hell out of me. I had no idea what was happening and worse yet, why.

Squad 2 broke the cherry. Other Squads in our unit started to deploy after we returned home. Like nothing happened, we went back to shift work. Back on nights after being in a combat zone, it is difficult to take the hype of security and vigilance seriously. The chances of something bad happening had decreased greatly. I tried to keep up with some of the things happening at the police department. I had heard my former supervisor had been moved to a different division and I would have a different boss when I returned to my duties at the police department. I did not look forward to going back to that toxic environment. Some, not all, of these supervisors were new and part of the crew that "did whatever they could to get ahead", movement.

I received a call from my new supervisor at the police department. This person told me that he needed my position filled immediately. I was informed that because I was not available, they would re-open the position that I had earned there, fill it with someone else, and put me back on the street as a patrol officer. I respect patrol officers, it's true law enforcement. I would be damned, though, if someone was going to move me out of my position as an investigator while on active duty. This was a perfect example of why I would never want to return to that type of environment. I resented the fact that my absence was merely a hole that needed plugging. I gave everything I had to this place, nearly my damn life on more than one occasion, and this was what mattered most? I had to get out of there, but not before I made some legitimate waves over this ignorant nonsense.

Someone, somewhere, for me it was a conspiracy between God and my wife, was looking out for my family. I was introduced to a senior federal official who arranged for me to partner with him at a federal agency. I was a direct hire and he immediately selected me from the list of candidates. This was the security I needed to educate one ignorant supervisor in regard to messing with soldiers on active duty orders.

My recourse was the local Judge Advocate General Attorney. I described the situation to that office. I don't know if it was a formal or informal conversation with the Chief of Police, but the day I told the JAG Attorney, I received an email from the Chief of Police at the time, assuring me that my position was guaranteed as I had left it when activated. He was apologetic and felt that someone maybe misspoke regarding the return of not only me, but other officers that were involuntary activated.

I am certain they didn't want this type of mess out in the media. I had that feeling in my gut and didn't believe a word in the email. I made sure my new employment was secured, but did not immediately tell the police department. I had it on good authority that the call from the JAG office caused a great deal of embarrassment for certain individuals. I also learned that it was the intention of the police department to eliminate my one investigator position, leaving me no choice but to return to patrol.

I had a new job I would be starting the day after I was released from active duty. It was time for my two weeks' notice at the police department. After a short career that seemed to span a lifetime of work, I looked down at the letter I was about to turn in to the city. All of the stories, tears, laughter, pain, and memories summed up in less than a paragraph. Most of the paragraph contained canned language regarding the date of my last day.

I walked through the halls of the police department saying farewell to our outstanding records staff. I was surprised when some shed tears. I think the tears were because they knew all too well I would not be the only one. I handed in my polyester uniforms, firearm, and all other issued gear. I asked if I could keep my badge or pay to have it mounted. The request was denied. That denial I took very personally. To me, it was a slap in the face and disrespectful. This was not the way I imagined how my career would end.

What they couldn't take were my memories. I walked to the main door, stopped, and took a deep breath. I looked out the security window that so many of the public looked in for help. I didn't look back. My vision began to tunnel and I could hear my heart beat in my ears. This building represented everything I was and it had changed in a terrible way. I was angry, hurt, and betrayed by the place where I had risked it all. This was no longer my department. I didn't want it. I pushed the heavy bar that released the lock with a loud click. I never heard the door slam as I walked out of the public entrance and away from the police department forever.

Goodbye Green

My departure from the police department corresponded with the end of my active duty orders. My enlistment had expired during my involuntary activation. When I was told I was being released from active duty, I gathered all of my issued gear that was to be returned and began out-processing.

I thought the out-processing would take days. Within a matter of about an hour, nine years of military service were over. There were no real goodbyes, no emotions, just a "thanks for turning your stuff in." This process was also very new to me. I did not realize the things that should have been done prior to my out processing. One important detail that was overlooked was an exit medical examination. This would not come to light until years later. My unit had never had to deal with active personnel like this in the recent past. Oversights were bound to occur.

Three months later there was a knock on our front door. A delivery person had left a box in front of the door and walked back to his truck. The engine roared as it sped down the avenue. This was a huge box, with stamps from several foreign countries. My wife walked into the living room.

"Oh my God, that is your care package I sent you almost 9 months ago!" She exclaimed.

I opened the package. The care she took in packing all of those items touched my heart. I would normally be upset at a lost package, but in this case, it was better late than never.

New Focus

My new federal position gave me the leeway to do things that seemed to suite my skill set. I was not a law enforcement officer in the traditional sense. The job series assigned to the position indicated law enforcement, however I primarily dealt with policy and administrative violations. I had a badge, a little authority, but no issued firearm. At first, this position was refreshing. The government salary was nearly double that of my police department pay. I didn't have the risks associated with the position that I had previously faced on a daily basis. It was Monday through Friday, holidays off. I did feel rather vulnerable, though. It was a nice break from true law enforcement and I absolutely hated every second of it. I wanted, needed to get back in to the game somehow. This office job would have to do until that day. That day would not come for several years.

On the Inside

Like a slow percolator, there was something brewing inside me. With every pump of coffee in the little glass lid, the closer I came to blowing mine. I don't know if this was the beginning, but it was definitely when things began to escalate. Internally, my rationale had become that absolutely no one was to be trusted. Going to the mall required a weapon, vigilance, watching people's hands and waistbands. This world is a dangerous place and I must always be prepared to react. This mindset was a safe way of thinking so that I could effectively protect my family from any potential evil that was surely lurking around every corner. Any presumed risk was out of the question. The thought of something happening to anyone I was responsible for was inconceivable. I was completely overprotective and hypervigilant for my sanity and family's sake. It seemed that two steps forward were always two steps back. For any deed presumed good, I would be punished with some sort of tragedy.

Friends? No friends other than my wife. Family was an exception but had to be watched with a close eye. I avoided any type of social event unless I was absolutely required to attend. I did not care to talk about police things or compare war stories with others. Around others, I would search for a hole to crawl into until it was time to go.

The simple act of obeying a traffic light or a stop sign became opportunities for bad things to happen. I constantly scanned the streets for danger regardless if I working or not. I naturally assumed that most drivers were not skilled and I had to be prepared to react in order to protect my family. I avoided the side of the road, keeping my vehicle towards the center. Bridges and traffic jams were like traps. Being surrounded on all sides with no escape became so concerning that my heart would race in my chest. I was constantly changing my driving routes and would go directly from my vehicle into the house. I hated living in town.

That is what was really going on. On the outside, people may not have noticed much of a difference, other than my tired eyes and impatient attitude. I was rather ultra-protective of my family. Risks were not an option. There were many triggers, some physical, many were verbal. "Chill out", "Relax", would often be offered to me. Those recommendations were met with a sharp and angry response. People offering the advice of relaxing obviously did not see what I could see. Whatever was happening was working because we were all still safe.

PART IV

The Agent

Federal Law Enforcement is quite different than policing an assigned beat for a department. From the training, to the clothes, to the work, becoming a Special Agent is a culture shock to those who had been on patrol. Special agents focus on programs for their respective agency, hence the name "Special Agent". Special agents have jurisdiction over programs or a certain part of the law. The amount of crime that occurs within those portions of the law typically involve numerous individuals in some sort of national or international scheme. The crimes may involve millions of dollars and cross over into another agency's jurisdiction. This was a job I wanted to do.

We wanted our son to have the opportunity to have an education in a system with smaller class sizes. It was the right decision. My wife aspired of living in the country on a small farm. Perusing the internet one day, I found such a place. Nestled in the rolling hills of Minnesota, sat a small farmstead with a white farm house. It had several out buildings and a large white barn. The driveway was about a quarter mile long, starting high, dipping downward and climbing back up a hill into the yard. From the picture window of the house you could see for miles. There was a lake at the end of the driveway and two large silos that once held feed for this once bustling dairy farm.

We placed an offer and it was accepted. Moving from the city into our new country lifestyle would be second nature to me. I had recently applied for a position as a Special Agent with the U.S. Department of Health and Human Services, Office of Inspector General (HHS-OIG). I knew that in the off chance I got the job, I would have to leave for several weeks of training. This training would likely occur during the winter months. Knowing my wife had never lived in the country, it was a definite concern. However, being in the country, with neighbors no closer than a mile away, was exactly what I needed and she wanted.

I traveled with another candidate to Kansas City, Missouri for the interview. Approximately two weeks later, I was told I was being selected for the position. My reservations of my wife being alone for the winter on a farm had not subsided. The person that would eventually become my supervisor admitted the interview panel had chuckled at the notion of two competing candidates riding all the way back to North Dakota in the same vehicle. It worked out, he was my colleague and already was an agent for another agency.

My wife is an amazing person. She eased my concerns about her surviving a cold winter alone on the farm.

"You need to do this. It's who you are" she said. Indeed, it is who I was and still am. She provided me a detailed plan of how her parents would live with her until I returned from

my training. I could always tell when she was unsure of herself.
When she professed her independence and told me everything
would be fine while I was gone, my fears and anxiety settled.
Just like that, I was back in the game.

<u>FLETC</u>

The Federal Law Enforcement Training Centers (FLETC) are
located in several geographical areas around the United States.
Glynco, Georgia was where I was headed to learn how to be a
law enforcement officer, again. Trading in the cool damp
weather of Minnesota, I arrived to be greeted with 90-degree
humidity and instant perspiration. This was definitely not a dry
heat.

With the exception of the weather and miles of almost
daily running, I excelled in this place. We were broken down
into two groups. Within those groups were smaller teams
consisting of about six to seven people. There were
approximately 40 potential agents in my class. The class was not
geared for a specific agency, so many of the students were from
a variety of agencies throughout the government. This was the
basic training portion; agency specific training would be
provided by each individual agency.

The uniforms we wore were dark blue with an embroidered patch indicating which program we were attending. Our patch had the Department of Homeland Security (DHS) logo and the letters CITP directly underneath. FLETC is a division funded and controlled by DHS. CITP stood for Criminal Investigator Training Program. The pants were dark blue with cargo pockets. These dark uniforms were probably not the best choice in the Georgia sun, but we got used to them.

Our rooms were dorms that shared a bathroom. FLETC is a former Navy blimp base with an interesting history. There was nothing fancy about the dorms, but they provided necessary shelter. Next to our dorm was the student center. This was a building that contained a well- utilized bar, juke box, pool tables, and a large room for Pay -Per -View events on the big screen. There were many near fights in that room during football season and UFC events. On Wednesday nights, there were karaoke contests. Two of my classmates shared victories on a regular basis. FLETC is pretty much self -sufficient and staffed with numerous professional men and women who call it their workplace. It takes up a large chunk of real estate near the Glynco Jet port.

The professionals that instruct at FLETC share their knowledge and skills acquired throughout their careers. I firmly believe that the majority of instructors genuinely care about student success. I was fortunate to have wonderful instructors. FLETC hires civilians to be role players. Whether it be interview training, arrest techniques, or other scenarios, these role players have a script and make the training as realistic as possible.

The firearms training division is a very busy place at FLETC. The number of students participating in training requires the schedule to be strict and efficient. The firearms staff have a no-nonsense attitude, and rightfully so. Accidents on a firing range can be incredibly dramatic and even fatal. I had extensive firearms training and was smart enough to keep my mouth shut about it. I let actions speak louder than words. Even if I was blowing the center of the target completely out, instructors would come up to me and give me shooting tips and advice. What I wanted to say was, "Geez thanks, but the person next to me is actually hitting my target, so maybe they could use some of your expertise." What I did say was, "Gosh, thanks, that is a really good point". It made me sick, but that was the best way to play it.

The driving courses were a great deal of fun. When the instructor tells you to drive the car like you stole it, you do just that. We were teamed up with a partner for the driving portion of our training. The tracks went for about two miles, maybe more. Winding and twisting turns required you to maneuver the vehicle at a high rate of speed, yet maintaining complete control. We wore helmets while driving these courses. For sanitary reasons, drivers were also required to wear a white hair net under their helmet as they were used by numerous students.

I was teamed up with a former state trooper from the southern part of the United States. He definitely knew how to drive. It was a Thursday morning when he and I mounted our vehicle. The night before, a class ahead of us had a small send-off party. There was that little hint of Maker's Mark still on his breath. He would be driving first and I was strapped into the passenger seat. There are certain people where the smell of certain booze just sticks with them. They are not drunk, you can just smell it on them the next day.

"Can you smell that?", he asked waving his hand in my direction. I did not respond. Producing a pack of gum, he took four to five pieces and began to chew. We sat with the windows down and waited for the radio to signal "go".

Staring straight ahead, not saying a word, the radio traffic came alive. The radio frequency was only one shared channel. It was patched into every instructor and every car. Instructors were stationed at different towers throughout whichever course was being utilized. They would call out car numbers and be giving way too much advice to drivers while the other instructors were trying to speak to other students. Drivers just had to listen for their car number for the commands from the instructors. We waited for our turn for our timed run. "23 go!" the radio blared. We sat looking straight ahead. "23 I said go!" the voice repeated. "I looked out the window and down at the large number on the door. Yup, we were number 23.

"Hey, I think he means us, there is a 23 on our door" I said. Without any warning, this former trooper's foot was to the floor and we shot off the starting line.

Like a snake on hot sand, we whistled around the track. Apparently, we were not supposed to pass slower cars, but this was a timed course. This guy knew how to drive. As we passed another student, the radio came alive scolding Car 23 and warning us not to pass anyone. The chatter on the radio was endless as we flew past the main tower, halfway through the course. He casually took his right hand off the wheel, reached down and clicked the radio off. We were flying and the turns were as smooth as a roller coaster. The smell of a hot engine and overworked brakes caught up with us on the last tight turn before the home straight away. The old trooper conducted some type of unauthorized drift maneuver that made up several seconds. I found we were perfectly in the center of the correct lane headed for the finish line.

We rolled into the pit area, no real expressions on our faces. I turned the radio back to the "on" position. One instructor came stomping up the driver's side window and poked his head inside. I don't know if it was the hint of a little Maker's Mark or maybe the sheepish look on both our faces. Before him were two former cops wearing mirrored sunglasses, hairnets, and safety helmets, who may or may not have smelled a little like blended Kentucky whiskey. He crinkled his nose and frowned, pushing his eyes to narrow slits. He shook his head and said,

"Jesus you guys, really?" His anger subsided when he got the time. It was one of the fastest in recent history.

"That was a great time, move on to skid control" he ordered.

"I think this radio is broken" I called out to the instructor.

"I sure as hell doubt that" he responded as he walked away.

A polished concrete pad with a constant glaze of moving water. Combined with nearly bald tires and you have yourself one of the most accurate representations of driving on icy roads that could possibly be simulated. In the trunk of the car was a device that would lock the brakes on either side effectively putting the car into an involuntary skid. This was going to be fun!

The radio sounded with speed and direction. I felt the brakes lock and the rear of the car starting to shift. I had three other students in the vehicle with me, all from California. I made a slight adjustment on the steering wheel and righted the car. Each time the instructor would lock one of the brakes, screams came from all of the passengers. This type of drill was something I had dealt with my whole life. Simple corrections ensured the car would right itself and everyone would be safe.

The passengers were struggling with a sense that the vehicle was out of control.

"Where are you from Sir?" the voice on the radio blared.

"North Dakota Sir", I responded. There was a short pause before the radio clicked again with an audible sigh. "Alright, let's see how many times you can make it go around!" the voice said.

I looked at my passengers with a grin. Their eyes were wide open and they were gripping on to anything attached to the interior of the car. Their heads were shaking side to side, indicating that this was one carnival attraction they would prefer not to ride.

"Now you're talking" I said. Finally, all of my years of go cart training as a child would pay off! I turned the steering wheel to the left and tried to push the gas pedal through the floor board.

The spin started slow. The view through the windshield began to blur the faster we began to spin. The screaming from the passengers was drowned out by my euphoric "Whoooooooooo!" I had lost count of how many rotations we had completed. I do know that not one of the passengers in the vehicle volunteered to ride with me ever again. My thought was, "I can't believe they paid me to do this. "

<u>Graduation</u>

I eventually graduated from FLETC. I received specific honors for marksmanship. I was on my way home to start my new career with my new agency. I had my own government car, badge, and gun. It felt great to be back doing what I felt I was best at doing. The agency didn't have my favorite programs that I would be investigating, but I was just happy to be part of the federal law enforcement community. There was more training in my future. I would have to complete my agency specific training which would include writing, program fraud, firearms, and protection detail training. In short, I would have spent a total of nearly 7 months training for this position.

<u>Work, Train, Work</u>

My agency specific training included writing, program fraud, firearms, and protection detail training. At some point I would also have to complete the Inspector General Academy training course. After a year and a half on the job, my required training had finally been completed. I had traveled back and forth to FLETC on three occasions for different training courses within that year and a half. I liked FLETC, but was sick of FLETC.

As I progressed in my career, I started to learn the tricks of the trade. Agents are accountable for every action. They are trusted certain freedoms and are typically treated like professionals. Agents are responsible for take home cars, several types of firearms, portable equipment, and tactical gear, just to name a few things. Abuse that trust and it is quickly taken away. Agents become masters of measuring personal liability with any potential legal ramification their actions may cause.

My agency assigned me as the second agent in a two-person office. This was perfect for me. I could be my angry and paranoid self and easily succeed at my job.

I gave my job my all. I was proactive in attempting to curb pain medication sale and abuse. I gave presentations when requested. I traveled wherever I was asked. Protection details would require us to travel and stay away from our families over holidays which was not such a bad break as I had become a rather argumentative person with my wife. We fought over some of the dumbest things. I cannot tell you how many times I thought of just walking out the door because I would just say whatever hurtful things I could to try and win an argument. I didn't want to subject her or our son to it anymore. Over and over, we would work it out at the last minute. I didn't know how they felt, but I knew I didn't feel much of anything.

I could not remember the last time I had genuinely laughed. When I traveled and was away from home, we got along best. I would be on the road or in the air almost weekly. When I was home for a day or two, things were fine. When I was home for a week, by about day five I would become annoyed at the slightest shift from what I wanted, needed, or expected. I am sure I made life hell for those around me. I had my reasons and did not want them questioned. In my mind there was one constant in my life, and that was work. In reality, the only constant in my life was the patience, understanding, and forgiveness of a loving wife and son.

Back to FLETC

I had been on the job for nearly a year and was told that I would need to go back to FLETC for agency specific training. I liked FLETC. The courses and life came easy for me. Like being deployed for the military, they house, feed, and clothe you. Your day is planned and there is little thinking involved regarding the small things in life. This training would consist of agency specific programs, report writing, driving, and protective services operations.

About half way through this training, I convinced my wife to come down and spend a long weekend with me. It would allow her to meet the people I spoke so much of as well as see the FLETC campus. The timing was perfect as she would arrive exactly half way through the training, which shortened up the time apart from one another.

For this particular training, we were housed at a local motel. This was great because while I was at training, my wife did a little snack shopping. She stocked the fridge and some drawers with snacks I rarely had time to purchase. We toured the campus, went shopping, and explored the South Georgia coast. I felt fortunate to have her there with me and enjoyed showing my classmates the woman of whom I spoke so much. Everyone loved her, especially the accent that comes with living in the northland.

When it was time for my wife to leave, she left a variety of the snacks she purchased. There was one particular kind of breakfast bar that I had not heard of, and one Saturday morning, I decided to try it. It was exquisite! I had slept through the hotel's complimentary breakfast so I gobbled up the breakfast bar. About ten minutes later, I found another of the same type of bar. I think I was becoming addicted to them because I ate that one with just as much enthusiasm.

My phone rang and one of my classmates wanted to head over to the local island as it was such a nice day. With nothing else on my weekend schedule, I grabbed a third breakfast bar, opened it, and ate it as I made my way down to my classmate's car. With my wrapper in hand, I sat down in the back seat and threw on my seat belt.

"What do you have there?" my classmate asked.

"Angie left them, and man are they great!" I answered.

"Oh, Fiber One bars, I have heard of them" he replied.

I learned a hard lesson that day. I did not realize that one Fiber One bar alone contains about 35% of the daily recommend amount of fiber for an adult. My stomach and intestines seemed to know this. About ¾ of the way to the island, the pressure moved from my stomach to my lower intestines. I didn't know what would happen if I submitted to the pressure. My guts were making horn type noises similar to an orchestra warming up prior to a performance. We had reached the beach and parked by a bathroom located in an elevated cabana.

I know that different tires take a certain pound per square inch, and I am certain I exceeded most Department of Transportation ratings. The cabana itself was built in almost a dome configuration. Wood floors, walls, and ceiling. Honestly, it would have made for the perfect sound environment for an acoustic show. My classmate who elected to stand outside, was treated to a chorus of sounds that he described as a tug boat coming to shore and a trombone on steroids. It didn't end there. It was hot, I was already sweating, and any relief of pressure was met with an equal replacement. I could not explain what was happening.

After about 10 minutes of my exclusive woodwind and brass ensemble- like concert, I felt some relief. I exited the cabana only to meet my wide-eyed classmate who was slowly shaking his head from side to side.

"Hey, you want one of these breakfast bars?" I asked.

"Hell no!" he exclaimed.

We made it about 100 yards down the beach and like a bad dream, it started all over again. The cabana would be too far, and there was no way I was going to run. The ocean was an option, but I was afraid of causing an Exxon Valdez size oil spill. There was one last option. I saw a security gate to a five-star resort that would be within hobbling distance. Without saying a word, I headed for it, formulating a plan on how I would get through the security gate.

"So, I will just wait here?" my classmate asked.

I didn't respond as it took everything I had to prevent my turbo charger from blasting me forward. As I reached the security gate, a nice old couple was using their access card to enter. I piggy backed them, greeting the security guard as if I was with the couple. I made my way down a short side walk and found a sign that indicated a restroom. There was a small band playing by the pool and the area with cluttered with several guests. Of course, keeping with an island theme, it was another cabana. I didn't care, and plowed my way past the bathroom attendant on the outside and through the door.

Much like after a severe storm, there is an eerie calm. Luckily, I was the only one in the restroom. My guts were finally at peace. As I walked out of the restroom, the attendant handed me a towel. I dried off my hands. He recommended I try the crab legs near the poolside bar. I thanked him and presented a dollar bill for his trouble. I know that a dollar was not enough as the first thing they should have done after that restroom visit would be to take a match and burn it to the ground. I sneaked out the gate and met back up with my classmate.

When I got back to the hotel later that day, I took all of the breakfast bars and threw them in the garbage. I have not eaten a Fiber One bar since.

The North Star

I spend a great deal of time traveling for work related activities. It may seem odd, but geography sometimes requires 8 to 10 hours of travel for one hour of quality work. We do what it takes to get the job done. We all are some sort of elite member at one chain hotel or another. Planning or travel typically revolves around necessity, holidays, and weekends. It is not uncommon for travel be 8 hours, do what is required, and then do the return trip the next day. This can happen week after week. Some colleagues enjoy homelife. This means they may choose to leave at 3 or 4 in the morning on a Friday for the sole purpose of getting home on a Friday.

I had traveled to meet a co-worker to do some liaison work. It was a Thursday, so I figured I would spend the night and leave early that Friday morning. I left the hotel at 4:30 with an estimated time of arrival at my home of 8:00 a.m. I jumped on the interstate and started my journey eastbound.

About 30 minutes into the trip, and four cups of coffee, nature decided I needed to pull into a rest area. I noticed a minivan at the rest area with what appeared to contain a single occupant. It was not necessarily out of the ordinary considering the rest area was on a major interstate. I climbed back into my car and merged onto the interstate.

There was not much traffic on the interstate at 5:00 a.m. It was late in the season and still dark. I noticed when I left the rest area, the minivan also left and followed me as I merged into the left lane. About 30 miles had passed and the minivan was tailgating me closely. I noticed a group of semi-trucks just ahead of me. I depressed the accelerator and saw I was traveling 100 mph. I intercepted the trucks, and the minivan kept pace. I managed to squeeze in between two trucks blocking the minivan and accelerated forward.

What was that all about? Another 50 miles had passed when I noticed a familiar set of headlights rapidly approaching the rear of my vehicle.

"What the hell?" I asked myself. I called my co-worker. I told him what was happening and that I would call Sheriff's Department in the county I would be soon entering. My co-worker told me to keep him updated should he need to dispatch the State Patrol.

The minivan was back on my ass. I saw an opportunity to conduct some deception. As I approached an overpass, I signaled I was exiting the ramp off the interstate. The minivan signaled the same intention. This exit was dark and led absolutely nowhere. I started to drift onto the exit ramp and the van followed. At the last minute, I jerked the wheel back to the interstate. Nearly clipping my rear bumper, the minivan sailed past and up the exit ramp. I flew under the bridge and continued eastbound.

I kicked the pedal to the floor and dialed 911. The dispatch assured me they would have a unit dispatched to intercept the minivan, but the unit was 40 miles away. I was traveling about 110 mph when I saw the same headlights approaching my vehicle. Now I was flat out pissed. I told the dispatcher my plan.

We were approaching a small town of which I was very familiar. Chances are, the person following me did not know the area like I did. I would travel by the school, double back and hide in a parking lot of a truck stop, away from the public. I would then confront the driver.

I hit the exit ramp I had described to the dispatcher at 100 mph. After a left and right turn, I was headed towards the school. The van was having difficulty keeping up with my maneuvers. I pulled down an alley and headed back towards an open parking lot by the truck stop. The van was losing ground and distance. I parked by a semi-truck and left my vehicle running. I hopped out of the vehicle and ran to the side of an unoccupied semi-truck. I saw the van coming and they were taking my bait. Safely away from pedestrians and children I watched as the van pulled in next to my vehicle.

I was on that driver faster than the driver could put the minivan in park. The driver, an older woman was staring at my vehicle and didn't even see me approach her, Glock. 40 pointed at her head.

"Police show me your damn hands!" I ordered. The woman did not have a chance. I had the drop on her. She did as I ordered. I removed her from the vehicle, patted her down, and began to field interview her. I was not happy, and my language was not that of a happy local patrolman. "What is your damn problem lady?" I asked. A small dog bounced from seat to seat in the vehicle barking at its master.

"I was told I had to follow the North Star to get home," she said.

Oh great, now I am the fricking north star. "Do I look like a star to you lady?" I asked.

"Why yes Sir, you are the north star and I am to follow you home." She responded. This was not making any sense. I had my flashlight and could see inside the minivan. The front two seats were accessible. The rest of the minivan was full of clothes and other items nearly to the roof. On the top of the pile in the minivan was a perfectly pressed baptismal gown. That was quite freaky.

"You do not move lady, do not move! You understand me?" I ordered.

"Yes, I do, North Star" she said.

When the county deputy arrived, I was relieved to see that it was someone I had known for a long time. After contacting her family, the deputy was able to ascertain that this woman had gone a bit under the wire. The family had been looking for her.

I found her, but it was more like she found me. The family said she had not been taking her required medication and often acted out on her delusional thoughts. I can only hope she was able to get the help she needed. She certainly picked the wrong vehicle to associate with the North Star. On this early morning, the situation nearly got her shot.

On a Peaceful Day

My sister –in- law's husband, Jeff, had been building my in-law's house. I would sometimes help him with certain projects during the construction. It was a cold day in Minnesota and I was taking a break from pouring a fireplace mantel. The work was hard but satisfying. The house had been coming along nicely and would likely be completed in the next month.

Jeff was a member of the local volunteer fire department. He wore that loud pager that would send a test tone every day at 6:00 p.m. It was around lunch time and I had grabbed a snack. My in-law's house is near ours and situated in the country. About two miles across the snow-covered fields runs a set of train tracks that head east and west. I could always tell when North Dakota oil production was in full swing just by the amount of train traffic. The oil production had recently decreased, and the trains only came by about every hour or so.

I was standing outside enjoying the calm of nature. Suddenly, the peace of the plains was shredded by a crash and the sound of crunching metal. I physically felt the earth shake beneath my feet.

"What the hell?" I asked outload. Moments later I could hear Jeff's pager screaming a familiar emergency tone. It was nowhere near 6:00 p.m. The message that came across Jeff's pager surely was meant for whatever I had just heard.

Jeff came tearing around the corner in his truck. "Train accident right over there!" he called as he sped by me. I jumped in my vehicle and sped after him. What I could see was that a train had stopped, blocking the rural intersection. About 200 yards to the west was what used to be a vehicle that the train had struck and effortlessly pushed until it had come to a stop. The truck was so mangled I could not tell the make or model. Jeff was headed down to the vehicle, and I was not far behind.

Jeff got to the vehicle first. He was half way in the window when I arrived. I saw what he saw. I saw what I had seen before in my career. Jeff turned and look at me. His eyes met mine as he slowly shook his head side to side. I knew what this meant. The driver had obviously not survived this violent crash. I ran back to the intersection while Jeff remained with the truck. As I reached the gravel road I spotted something that stopped me dead in my tracks.

"Please God not that, please god no!" I mumbled to myself. Lying face down on the side of the embankment was a child's car seat. I didn't want to but had to. I ran to the car seat and slowly turned it over. Empty, it was empty. I searched the area hoping if a child was in the seat that they were not ejected.

Thankfully, there did not appear to be a child anywhere around the area. Then I spotted the next item.

I had a government emergency vehicle. I had parked it in the middle of the road with the emergency lights flashing wildly. I remember seeing something strange when I first arrived, but between the mangled vehicle and car seat, I didn't take the time to check it out. It was a propane tank in the middle of the road just in front of my vehicle. Below the propane tank was a piece of paper. I walked over to the tank, cautiously inspecting it as I approached. I tilted the tank and slid out the paper that was wedged between the tank and road.

I read the letter. The letter was about fear, love, and heartache. The letter was addressed to a family. It explained where and when it was written. The hard part to read was "the why" it was written. I was reading a small snapshot of a person's life. The letter described how a once vibrant life became too much, leaving the author in shambles. Lastly, it was an apology to a family for everything.

This was not an effort to make things right, it was a suicide note. This person felt that committing suicide would make things right for them. What it did was require a bunch of people to clean up a mess. I felt for the conductor of the train who was helpless to prevent this intentional act. I think about that day every time I cross those tracks.

Betrayed

A measure of success for Agents is when they have achieved a journeyman paygrade. This is the highest, non-supervisor paygrade available to most agents. Each agency has a different evaluation criterion to achieve this pay grade. It was a cold November when my supervisor gave me the call. He congratulated me on my successful selection to the journeyman grade. This meant I was truly an adult and would receive a pay increase. It was one of the greatest days of my life.

My life, oh yeah, I forgot about that. I forgot how this plays out. I forgot that there is a price to pay for everything. No good thing goes without having to pay some sort of toll. I just wondered what tragedy would be lurking out there.

It was just before Christmas that year when I received my second call from my supervisor. This was to inform me that those in upper management had decided that we had done such a great job, our skill would best suit the agency in a more populated area, permanently. In short, they were closing our office and involuntarily moving us to a location to be determined by those much smarter than us.

This was not happening! It was devastating news and the reasoning was absolutely absurd. I had not had a Merry Christmas in years. This year would be no exception.

What Now?

Cops get to tease other cops, even in the most unusual ways. Cops can crack jokes and share sarcastic comments that would make most people so uncomfortable, they would want to stand up and leave the room. Attorneys do not get to make jokes at cops that way.

Part of an office closure is to notify everyone who the action may impact. The news of our office closure was going over like the popular turd in the prom punch bowl, yet no one really cared. My co-worker and I notified one official regarding our office closure. He didn't even seem mildly interested that two agents were leaving the district. Other officials expressed displeasure, however, and even wrote letters to the agency. This particular official took a different approach. His office was in the middle of a remodel. The official looked even smaller than he was behind the big desk that appeared to be new, or just polished from lack of use.

The official said, "Hey, I have a job for your guys, they need help pulling up the carpet over there" and then chuckled. It took everything inside me not to reach across the desk and fold this person like a paper airplane and fly him out the window. That small mind in that small body must have thought he'd cracked a joke. I wanted to show him what a crack really sounded like. Karma rears its head at the most opportune times, and surely Karma was listening this day.

My co-worker applied for and was hired by a different agency. Fortunately for him, it was back in his home town. I was glad it worked out. I was job hunting on a daily basis. Finally, I found a similar position with another agency that would be stationed in Minneapolis, MN. This was not an ideal situation, but we could make it work. I applied for and interviewed in person for the position. Speaking with the supervisor and the Special Agent in Charge was as if I had known them my whole life. The questions were easy and I felt right at home. The position would not be where I lived, but I could manage a hotel or whatever needed to be done just to remain an Agent. I called my wife on my way home and told her the interview went well. "I would be absolutely astonished if I do not get selected for this position" I said.

About a week had passed. I was at my brother's farm helping him with harvest. My phone rang and it was the supervisor from the agency where I had just completed interviewing. He told me that he appreciated my application and interview, but I was not selected. I couldn't believe it. How is that even possible? I was so close to fixing this problem yet now I have to start over. My family is in jeopardy and I can not make things better. The depression, stress, and anxiety were killing me inside. My current agency had invested a lot in my training, and yet, they were still willing to throw all that away. I couldn't stay there after that betrayal.

Three months of hell had passed and my current agency established a deadline for complete office closure. Three months and one day, my phone rang. It was the Special Agent in Charge with whom I interviewed previously. He offered me a position with his agency in a different, and much better location. Still not ideal, but even better than the first. I could not believe it. A solution with little time to go.

"Thank you, God!" I exclaimed. It was not the best scenario, but I could make it work. The office would only have one other agent, just like before. The programs were less subjective. Best yet, now I got to be a passive aggressive jerk until my final day with my current agency.

The politics that an Agent deals with are eye opening. It takes some time to get the feel for exactly how to speak, act, and see political decisions that may affect you. Once an Agent figures out the ins and outs, others see them as almost clairvoyant. There are often limited outcomes to political actions. By watching and listening, it almost becomes easy to predict the probable outcomes.

This office closure was becoming politically unpopular. After I was long gone, someone would have to answer for the decision to close this office. I guess the majority of those who made the decision would try and leave before they were rewarded with a post of duty somewhere unpleasant. I found out later, that is exactly what had happened with the exception of one, who was left to answer for it all. Karma visited and that made me smile.

<u>The Day Before</u>

My parents were snow birds. They spent their summers in a West Fargo, ND twin home and their winters in the Southern Valley of Texas. I visited them the day before I was to report to my new post of duty. Another agent sent me a text message regarding another position in my agency. I pulled up the government's job site and saw that the agency had posted the exact same position I had applied for and accepted, now available in my home area as well. Home, that is where I wanted to be. What strange timing.

It was one of the most uncomfortable calls I ever had to make. I had to call my new supervisor and explain to him about this new position in my home state versus the position of which I was to report for the next day. I was a lucky guy. My new supervisor was a kind and compassionate man, almost too nice to be a boss. He told me that he completely understood and would speak it over with the management. I about wore out my parent's carpet as I paced back and forth waiting for the return call.

"Report for duty as ordered and we will work on getting you home, Son" my new supervisor said. I thanked him and the management staff profusely. I slumped in my chair and let out a big sigh. "This agency really cares about their people", I thought.

Priceline was an amazing tool. I would get up at 3:30 a.m. on Monday mornings, pack up the food my wife placed into individuals meals, and head the four-hour drive to my new office. I stayed in a hotel for the week and would come home late Friday evening. I was missing the majority of my son's baseball games, but we were making it. We paid for my hotel every week. I worked hard and waited for that call that told me I could go home. We had to hire a new agent before I could return home forever.

After eight long months, we hired another agent. The government is large, but this corner of the world is a small. The candidate was an experienced and would have no problem catching on to how things worked. I knew the candidate well. As expected, they sailed through the process. I provided them information on what I had learned in my short eight months. My supervisor called and told me that he was coming for a visit with the Special Agent in Charge. Upon their visit, they told me if I could acquire some free, low cost, or joint office space, I could move back home permanently. They had me at home.

I had office space secured in a matter of two phone calls. It would be temporary, but it bought me time. I left that office, walked to my car, and never looked back. I was on my way back home. Grateful, blessed, lucky are just a few words that described this opportunity. I would not let them down. I was going to be working with Agents from other agencies of which I was familiar. Back home, I knew everyone-- attorneys, judges, and local law enforcement.

I received a nickname on my first day back. One of the Homeland Security Agents came to the office and shook his head. "Well, well, well, look who they tried to do in and is back" he said. "They tried to you knock you out of the tree and yet here you are" he said laughing. I thought it was rather amazing myself. "You are just like a cat, they push you out, but then you land on your feet" he roared.

This had been pretty accurate thus far. When I call him to this day, there is no "Hello" or "Hey there!" Instead I am greeted with "What's up cat?" I am just fine with that nickname. I really needed to take note of how many of my 9 lives I had used.

Predictability

I have rarely had to work in an office with more than one other person. Collateral duties for most positions involved paperwork and other recurring reports. I was able to do the majority of my work from behind a keyboard and computer screen. Phone calls were minimal and so was my interaction with anyone outside the family. This position allowed me to become a unique type of agent. A lone wolf on the prairie focused on whatever needed to be done. My domicile was geographically placed perfectly in an area that had seen little coverage. Allowing me to work from domicile reduced travel time for others, to include overnights. This was too good to be true, yet there I was.

Agents are a different breed. Quite eccentric and not wanting to be uncomfortable for extended periods of time, they find creative ways to get the job done. They have the ability to focus in on the small details and tenaciously expose any amount of dishonesty. Time and resources that are not usally available to patrol officers, allow Agents to concentrate on a fraud specific to their agency.

Granted, most agencies have several hundred programs, some of which most have never heard of before. Each program, regardless of agency, has different rules and regulations. There was no way to know all the details of each specific program.

The fact of the matter is, the goal is the same, the badge is different. Same players, different game. Once you have played the game, it takes just a little tweaking to hit the ground running wherever you land. Like a merry go round, my federal career had come full circle. From great, to terrible, to not so terrible, and now back to where I was most comfortable. My feelings towards the world had not changed. My perception of good versus evil had never been more slanted. I trusted no one because that left me vulnerable. I continued to have a short temper. I was angry and it was affecting my life. I was just waiting for the moment to have it all taken away. History had taught me that in time, I would have to defend everything that was now my life. I found it hard to be a happy person when all I could think about is what battle would be next.

Undeniable Proof

I do not criticize other's beliefs, for the most part, but personally I believe in a sixth sense. That feeling of electricity that brings your senses to life. It feels like you almost know something is going to happen, so your body starts physically and mentally preparing to act. Documenting certain events of my life, I would be hard pressed to say there was not a higher power. I have seen some pretty amazing things in my life and in my fellow humans. I have also witnessed horrors that made me question why a higher power would allow them to happen. My conclusion is that I don't know. I don't know why people shoot our children in schools. I can't explain why a family is killed by a drunk driver. All I can do is trust that things happen for a reason, no matter how horrible. I also have to look at how many things are averted. Some may call it luck, I call them miracles.

I was standing on an indoor firing range with several other shooters some time ago. It had been a long week, and this was a great way for me to unwind. I was most comfortable shooting and dealing with guns, even though it is not my favorite thing to do. I do enjoy volunteering where I can be of help. This day though, something was just off. The electricity had been building inside me all day. I had that feeling deep down inside, moving about my guts like a slow river. Like a good cop, I was breaking minor firing line policies by looking at messages on my telephone while standing on the firing line. Finally, the last shooter appeared to be finishing his remaining ammunition. I had sent my wife a message and told her I would call her just after we finished.

I was rather disinterested with what was happening in front of me. I was not instructing, just a shooter at a range, a nobody, and it was a nice change of pace. My hearing protection had microphones so that I could hear sounds, but when they were over a certain decibel, the noise was muted to safe levels.

I heard my text tone sound. I glanced around the firing line and turned to grab my phone.

The explosion was not that of a traditional firearm. I heard it before I felt it. It sounded like pebbles being tossed about the firing line. I felt the impact in my left shoulder and left wrist. I was pushed forward slightly. My shoulder became hot and my right wrist was on fire. The pain was not far behind. What felt like a swarm of bees stinging me all at once, was shrapnel from a negligent discharge of a shotgun. The shrapnel made its way quickly down the line, penetrating anything soft.

I turned around and saw one of the people on the line taking a knee, blood rushing from his arm. Another person was on the ground reciting every swear word in the English vocabulary. My shoulder and wrist felt like someone was holding a lighter within inches of both. What I learned is that when people are trying to help, sometimes it makes matters worse. One of the people tried to brush the shrapnel from my shoulder, effectively pushing it in further. I removed my shirt and it hung on my shoulder from the shrapnel. It reminded me of how a sock gets caught on a sharp toenail.

Luckily no one was seriously hurt. I could see that the shooter was completely distraught. It had to be humiliating, terrifying, and a horrible memory to face. I do know that it was a miserable feeling having that hot shrapnel in my shoulder and right wrist area. If I had not turned to check my text message from wife, I would have been hit in the left side of my face and the exposed portion of my neck.

Three months after this incident, I took a week off for a hair band festival. We attend this festival every year. Where else can you share an elevator with Lita Ford or perhaps the band Warrant? We were at one of the shows and decided to go back to our camper for some refreshments. As I sat in my lawn chair, my right wrist would not stop itching. I thought a mosquito had enjoyed some of my rum- laced blood. I went to the table inside the camper and gave my wrist one last scratch. A faint but audible metallic sound hits the table. I believe that was the last piece of shrapnel from incident on the range.

PART V

The Advocate

The situations that fate has dealt me is not a question, it is the result of what has transpired in my life. This is what I am and what I am learning about. This is what has consumed people of whom I used to be close, and it has taken them from this world, forever. These are my demons and I am no longer afraid nor embarrassed to share them with anyone. I am a young man with many years to live, yet I write these stories because I want other young men and women to know that they also have a long life ahead of them. Not just a long life, but a life filled with peace, love, and happiness. These things once existed for me, then disappeared for years. I am just recently starting to try and find them again. It's hard and takes deliberate actions to make it work. Being angry and paranoid daily takes more energy than to try and find peace of mind. Make it a goal to live in the peace you have protected, fought for, and earned.

Getting What I Deserve

One major obstacle I still deal with looks a lot like happiness, but it isn't. I struggle the most around my birthday and throughout the entire Christmas season. What exactly do I deserve? I am the last person on earth that will look at something and tell my self I have earned that. I rarely feel I have done enough to earn anything that could bring potential joy to my life.

When the kids open their gifts during our family holiday, I feel a profound sense of happiness. When I see packages with my name on them, my first thought is someone wasted their time and money. They could have got the kids something else. I know I am not alone stating that I do not feel I need or deserve kindness given by others. I would prefer to give than receive. This all makes me feel quite uncomfortable.

I was once told, "Good things happen to good people." For most part, I can see that is true. Maybe it is my slant on the world, but that is not the case for me. I am not trying to be a whiner or complain, but this phenomenon has been a consistent pattern throughout my life. The pattern is so apparent, my wife now also has begun to notice it, which is likely my fault. I am grateful for our home, family, health, food and other necessary essentials for a good life. I am always very leery of anything above that. If things are falling into place and my day, week, or month is just going great, I have learned that there is a cost. That cost comes in the form of something that will take away from the joy that I experience. Like a ball bouncing on concrete, every action causes and equal and opposite reaction. Maybe it is fate, maybe luck, but when good things happen, they are hard to enjoy because the impending doom that follows soon after lingers like a bad leg cramp. Enjoying the simple things in life is safe, but I am now always prepared to pay with my emotional check book. The way I see it, I get what I deserve.

No Way to Live

Vigilance is a noble trait often associated with heroic acts of valor. It is also an important tool for law enforcement and military personnel to help keep you and your partners safe. Vigilance is a double edge sword. There needs to be a switch. A person has to be able to turn it off. I did not have an off switch. Providing a sixth sense type of perception, vigilance gives a step up on the competition. In the competition of life, the difference between winning and losing can be fatal. In the long term, not having the ability to turn it off can also be fatal.

I was driving my family nuts. Everywhere we would go, I was armed. Before I walked into a building, I took mental notes of people, things, anything out of the ordinary. Taking a mental security survey of the building, finding exits, bathrooms, and other areas that may need to be used at a moment's notice, I was constantly ready to respond to a variety of events that may present themselves.

Now don't get me wrong, I am typically always armed to this day, primarily for personal protection. I have earned that right. However, torturing oneself over what may happen with a never-ending list of possible scenarios is constant torment. It is a game no one can possibly win. If you go to the store and prepare for a robbery to happen while you are shopping and it doesn't, it is thrown in your mental trash. If the robbery does occur, it only supports the notion that no one is to be trusted and you should be giving psychic readings.

The problem that I had was there was a greater than average likelihood that one of those scenarios could come to fruition. When a situation would occur, it would only reinforce my belief that I was either psychic or a magnet for disaster. Just so you know, I cannot talk to the dead or read a palm. But my senses did tell me that this was no way to live.

<u>Crowded Places</u>

Certain things reinforce my beliefs. Two steps forward in an attempt to reduce the hypervigilance, and then there is an incident that moves me three steps back.

I hate crowded places. I do not care for unorganized large groups of people. I don't find these situations safe and need to be watching everyone to ensure that there are no threats.

I need to know where all of the zones are located so I can advance in case of an emergency. In short, it is the old police adage: "Smile, be nice, and have a plan to kill everyone in the room."

An example of my hypervigilance has even taken place in my hometown Walmart. Situated on Highway 10 in Detroit Lakes, Minnesota, Walmart is a busy store most of the year. On a quiet afternoon, my wife and I had a few items to pick up prior to heading home for the evening. I do not like standing in lines for many reasons. Here we are, minding our own business on a quiet weekend. Soon we are being shuffled to the front door because there was a threat of a bomb. Neither my wife nor I were surprised that this occurred when all I wanted to do was buy some new razor blades.

Concerts, also, have been a particular challenge for me. I don't mind the 10,000 people standing in front of me, it is the other 25,000 behind me that I cannot see, who worry me. Every concert I've attended, I seem to be placed next to some moron that thinks they need to show the lead singer that they have a beer, holding it above their head. As beer splashes like a lawn sprinkler over everyone in a 10-foot radius, I feel I need to chew their ass. I really don't want to but it needs to be done. If I don't lecture them, my wife will, and she likes to fight. God I love her. I also like a good scrap but like the Toby Keith song goes, "I ain't as young as I once was."

Feeling

Feelings of love, happiness, and being settled left me years ago. I do care and have love for my family. I mean, I have an operational plan prepared simply to go get fuel for a lawnmower. But when asked what makes me happy, I struggle to answer. Once the silence was broken, I respond that being left alone makes me happy. Not having to meet new people outside of the professional realm makes me happy. Not having to answer questions about personal things makes me happy. Not going to crowded places where people ask the questions like, "What's the worst thing you have seen?" or "Have you ever had to kill anyone?", makes me happy. I don't even respond to questions like that and search for an exit. Not having to explain myself or have small talk with anyone would be a gift.

Looking back at my answers to that question raises a level of irony. The things that I responded that made me happy were actually avoiding things that make people happy. I obviously have a level of distrust for most people. I am curious as to what angle someone is playing when interacting with me. I listen to their voice and if speaking in person, analyzing their body language.

Numb is a good description. Lack of empathy and believing the world is not this beautiful paradise where a lot of the other people live their protected lives, was how I thought.

When I said I didn't care, I truly did not care. I know what love is and I tried to give it. I know what fear is and I understand it. I also know what anger is; I know I can feel it. My organizational skills regarding emotions have been misplaced and I search for them daily.

My nonprofessional theory is that the terrible arguments I would have with my wife made my blood boil. I could not tell you many of the topics that were so important at the time. I would do anything to get a reaction from her, hoping in the end, we would embrace and be closer than ever. During the argument I felt anger, fear, but at the end of each heated argument, I felt a little glimmer of something that had been missing, and that was love. It wasn't a permanent feeling, but I was so frustrated and confused at what was happening to me, I needed to feel loved. What I didn't realize was that I was loved, more than ever. I was just too blind to see it in front of my face.

Riding Shotgun

If you do not like to drive, you and I will get along famously in a vehicle. I have learned to conceal my anxiety very well over 20 years. Riding as a passenger should be a relaxing experience. Riding as a passenger for me is an opportunity to constantly scan our surroundings for potential danger. There are

very few people I can stand to be in a car with as a passenger.
The simple thought of having to experience this will keep me up
the night before. This includes cars, trucks, boats, and airplanes.
I am not a pilot, but I am pretty sure if they gave me a fake yoke
or stick to simulate me flying the plane, I would feel much
better.

Just let me drive and we will get along just fine. Another
strange thing about being a passenger in a vehicle is that it puts
me closest to the side of the road. The side of the road contains
dangers. For some, it was road side bombs, children running out
in front of cars, or simply going in the ditch to avoid an accident.
I do not like sitting closest to the side of the road.

One morning while riding to school with my brother in
his 1978 Thunderbird, we had a little mishap. Slush had caused
the front wheels of the car to hydroplane out of control. The last
thing I heard him say was, "Were going in". Go in we did,
Dukes of Hazzard style. In a time before kids had cell phones,
we had to rely on good neighbors.

A neighbor working in his yard saw us leave the ground
and land in the bottom of the water filled ditch, narrowly missing
a stop sign. I hit my head on the dash. The impact bent the
frame on the big car. The sound of the vehicle hitting the ground
was violent. The follow up thump I could only assume was my
head contacting the dash. I still remember that Bon Jovi was
playing on the radio as we did our best Dukes of Hazzard

impersonation that day. I am grateful it was not a worse situation. My Guardian angel surely suffers from anxiety.

<u>Anxiety</u>

If you have worked in any emergency services occupation, you have experienced several degrees of anxiety. Anxiety is definitely present my life most days. People that know me are reading this and probably shaking their heads. I am known as a cool headed, informed decision maker. I have not quite learned how to cope with anxiety but have a PHD in hiding my mental and physical reaction to whatever triggers my symptoms. For me, there are two types of anxiety that I battle.

There is the known stressor that will happen in the future, like being a passenger in a vehicle. Then there are the possible or ambiguous stressors like having to sit in traffic for great lengths of time or traveling to an unknown area and not driving the route prior to my actual trip.

My ambiguous stressors are like a game of pin the tail on the donkey. They come in blind and surprise me. I may not know what they are, but when they hit me it causes a physical reaction, typically involving my digestive system. I sometimes learn of these new triggers as they occur. Most recently I found my hatred of car washes and elevators. I know some can relate to this as being confined puts me in a defensive mode.

I didn't know what was happening to me was a panic attack. The panic attacks I had seen on television involved some hysterical person bouncing off the walls only to be hauled away to a padded room by large orderlies. That description may be true for some, but it is quite the opposite for me. I sit quietly as my mind processes completely illogical thoughts. These thoughts can be so outlandish that in hindsight, they are not even realistic. Physically I see stars, my vision begins to narrow, my breathing starts to accelerate. My heart starts to beat at an abnormal pace and I feel almost static electricity all over my body. I get hot, and start to sweat. Lastly, I can either smell or hear things that I normally wouldn't be able to identify. It is scary as hell, but sitting next to me, you may not know it is happening unless for some strange reason I would have ahold of your arm or hand. You may speak to me, and I will hear you, but not hear what you said. My Grandpa Elmer used to do that to my Grandma Doris, but I am pretty sure it was intentional.

If anyone does anything I may perceive as out of the norm during these incidents, they receive extra mental scrutiny from me. I go into survival mode and prepare to get through whatever situation may present itself. More often than not, almost always, nothing happens and it is a created fear in my mind. This is my panic attack, and I live with them frequently. Unfortunately, my family also is on the receiving end of some colorful behavior and language that I supply during these situations. It is very easy to become overwhelmed. There are techniques to reduce this, but I have yet to master them. Luckily my family has been forgiving and patient.

<u>Patience</u>

I am a huge fan of late 1980's metal music. I love the band Guns n' Roses. Their song "Patience" meant little to me growing up. As I listen to the song now, I truly start to believe that I could use a little more patience. I have lost patience for most things, which I do not make any attempt to conceal. I have a short list of things that I make a conscious effort to give patience towards. I have patience for most young children. Children get a pass because of their innocence in the world. I find peace in listening to children describe their days, things they have built, and the stories they tell.

Veterans have earned my respect and I genuinely enjoy listening to them as they describe the bits and pieces of their lives. Elderly people have also earned my respect. The stories and experiences are not only entertaining but almost always contain some sort of wisdom. Like a parable from the Bible, the elderly never stop teaching until they take their last breath.

Animals also get my respect. They trust us to take care of them. We trust animals to take care of us. Our animals are an important part of our family. They are one of the few things in this world that can calm my warrior attitude.

Not that anyone cares, but able body adults get little or no sympathy from me. I find their problems to be mostly excuses and their pain a whining that is most often because of their own lack of action. There are exceptions to this, however. If people have just not taken control of their lives and are now complaining about it, I will go sit at the kids' table because it is much more interesting.

As these symptoms grew, I found I started to become easily annoyed at small things. The slamming of car doors, fireworks, loud eaters, people dragging their feet on carpet, and gum smackers. People who come to your home and their cell phone rings and they start a loud conversation with someone, only to tell you to be quiet. I still intentionally make all the "accidental" noise I can at that point. Or worse yet, loud eaters. I cannot stand the sound of open mouth chewers or loud eaters. I literally have to get up from the table and drive to the next county. Unfortunately for me, I am surrounded on both sides by a family of loud eaters.

Last, but definitely not least, are liars. With telling half the story in an attempt to manipulate facts or flat out lying, I have no patience. We always told our son to tell the truth, no

matter what. We will work through whatever it is, but do not lie.
There are few things more hurtful than when people around you,
intentionally mislead others by fabricating truths or leaving out
key pieces of information that mirrors but does not tell the truth.
This happens on countless occasions and has changed many
relationships. When that line gets crossed even one time, it
changes everything. Like the comedian Steven Wright said, "I
live at the end of a one-way dead-end street." Don't travel down
that street because there is no way to turn back.

I am Not Interested

As a person's life progresses, so do priorities. Hobbies
used to be an important part of my life. I loved hunting, fishing,
shooting, basketball, and a variety of other activities that
occupied my free time. I no longer hunt, hate basketball, and
typically only shoot when I have to qualify. The last time I was
fishing it lasted about 10 minutes. I ended up bobbing in the
water on an inflatable stingray drinking a beer. The thought of
me having to get up early to walk a frozen shelter belt for a deer
is the last thing I would like to do on my day off. My dogs
dislike gun shots and that works just fine for me.

I used to set my watch to whatever time COPS was on
television. Now I avoid any type of police show. Major credit

goes to the officers because I would not have the patience to deal with the drunk guy on the park bench like I used to do so many years ago. It is a very difficult job and they deserve praise for keeping their heads about them shift after shift.

Recent war movies are something I intentionally avoid and have lost any interest even in hearing the plot. These types of films are typically tragic, cause anxiety for me, and are somewhat predictable. I honor our veterans every chance I get. I also think it is important to have good quality movies as I just described. Watching them for me is not something I care to ever do, however.

<u>**Depression**</u>

Most have had that drunk friend. You know the one, they get one or two drinks in them and they start reminiscing about a past relationship or that perfect weekend at the lake. Soon after they are drunk texting their ex-girlfriend or boyfriend three times over and tears start rolling like an oil lamp. Combine that with sad music playing in the background and you have just written a country music hit. Just so you know, I don't have much patience for that either. It is very uncomfortable for me. I didn't know much about depression until recently. I asked a psychologist one day, is it possible to have depression and be a comedian? She smiled and answered, "One of my favorite comedians was Robin Williams". Then it began to make sense to me.

I am not a doctor and I can only describe my observations. For me, depression is like a demon, hiding deep in someone's inner core. It lingers there and unlike anxiety, slowly builds and then creeps out. Before you know it, it has consumed you and the battle is underway before you have even loaded your gun. Like a short stack of pancakes, multiple situations pile on top of each other. What I have learned, each pancake may not be as important as another pancake, but stack all the pancakes together, and soon you have a pile. Depression can cause your entire thought process to change. Your body and actions tend to follow these perceptions. This can definitely have a profound effect on anything you do.

Depression and anxiety can masquerade as creative abilities when it comes to the arts. It is likely that some of the best poems, songs, and literary works came from the deep feelings or emotions from their authors. Commercials play upon our emotions, but get someone battling depression watching an ASPCA commercial with music by Sarah McLaughlin, and the tears can start rolling. My wife does not suffer from depression, but covers her ears with her hands and head with a blanket during those commercials.

The symptoms of my depression come and goes. It is more of a notion that anything negative that happens in my life is my fault. Perhaps maybe I am being punished for something. Accepting is believing that particular notion is a part of my depression.

I faded away from those of whom I used to have any sort of friendship. I intentionally avoided military and law enforcement colleagues. Sure, I would run into people here and there. We would give each other the same old chit chat most people offer one another, but there was no authentic sharing. I did not want people to feel obligated to have to come and speak with me. This was on me. These are good people, I just didn't want to interact with anyone. I would make the rare exception if the conversation was prefaced with a hearty rumor or gossip.

Not Sleeping and Forgetting Things

I legitimately thought I was experiencing the early onset of Alzheimer's disease. Memories were stored in my brain like a disorganized closet. I am typically a very organized person. I started to find myself forgetting small things in life. My short-term memory was taxed and it became very frustrating. I would lose my keys several times a day. I could not remember names or addresses. Thank god for my password book or I would never get in to my Amazon account. I would often forget what day of the week it was. Focusing and concentrating on work was exceptionally hard.

I found myself day dreaming very frequently. I would be staring at a fixed object and my wife would either snap me out of it or another stimulus would alarm me. Sometimes ten minutes would pass before I would come back to reality. I was tired a great deal of the time because I either woke up or was not be able to go back to sleep or just not sleep at all. My mind did not seem to have an off switch. I sometimes have had vivid dreams, nightmares, or short and intense thoughts that seemed as if they were happening over and over again.

Images of events scatter though my head, often when day dreaming. They are vivid and seem real. Pictures scattered all over a room blowing around like one of those grab the cash machines at a casino. A flash here, another there, and so on. There is no rhyme or reason to the order in which they appear.

It is important to work on taking these things out of that disorganized closet, labeling them, and packing them back in a fashion that is manageable. It may take a lifetime to accomplish. It is a confusing thing to have this happen. I especially struggle with images and forgetfulness to this day. (An inside tip: if you are looking for a sound investment, post it notes may be a great opportunity for you. I use my share to simply organize my activities on a daily basis.)

Anger, Taking it Personally

I struggle with the battle of good versus evil. I don't like to lose, and I certainly do not like it when an injustice is rewarded instead of punished. It doesn't take much to get me angry. A small stimulus triggers a response. Backed into a corner, I will come back at you in survival mode. It is either there, or not there. There is no middle ground. There is no zero to ten. There is only about five and 10. Anything perceived as a threat or intentionally harmful is met with an immediate and aggressive response. Small things that are simply part of life can be perceived as personal attacks on me.

When I speak of anger, I am not talking about a temper tantrum. I am speaking about going into warrior mode, doing and saying whatever it takes to get a reaction. Blood boiling anger where destroying whatever caused it is a primary focus. The amazing thing is that about a day later, I was sometimes hard pressed to remember what I was so damn mad at.

Any deviation from a plan I developed is also a personal act of disrespect. I would do everything in my power to protect me and my family. If you were not with that plan, you were against it and a threat. The most simple and general deviation from my thought process is a complete personal attack and would need to be dealt with swiftly. I would not stand for a second attempt on victimizing my family or anyone I have taken an oath to defend.

The energy involved in dealing with these perceived personal attacks has kept me up at night and distracted me during the day. I would plot and scheme to get even or place barriers to prevent future situations from affecting me. *How dare people even consider crossing this path with me? How dare they?* I would think to myself.

This rationale was chipping away at me day after day. All of the perceived threats were way too much stimulus to deal with and I didn't feel anyone else was doing enough to prevent events from occurring. I was exhausted.

Surrendering and Forgiving

I learned that I do not like the idea of surrendering to anything. I do not like to lose. According to my Facebook feed, it was exactly one year ago today when I had a talk with my wife. I had been off for about two days, having to do something I really had not wanted to do. I was passive aggressive and quiet. If someone would have described my behavior, they would have said that bald headed guy was pouting.

We spoke very little on the way home. The feeling of darkness, being alone, and exhausted, flooded me to my core. For the first time in 20 years, I truly opened up to my wife. I told her I felt like shit, pretty much all the time. I proceeded to talk continuously for about three hours during our drive home from Minneapolis. I started from the beginning and took her to the present. I had to surrender to the notion that it was probably time we took a look at how I operated. I didn't realize that she was already an expert in that field. That day changed my life, but it wasn't over yet. I had to accept things for what they were and ask her to forgive me for who I had become.

I also do not like the notion of forgiveness. It's a hard thing to think and even say. Sometimes to get it right, it has to be said several times. In order for me to keep my family and sanity, I was going to need to evaluate some of my perceptions that in my mind, that had kept me alive. I would need to try to surrender the notion that everyone in the world was evil and out to damage me and my family. I would need to let my child do things that I perceived as risky. I would have to listen instead of give advice. I would have to step back. That is hard to do for someone who is passionate about stepping forward.

This change in me is not happening overnight. For me surrendering and forgiveness are a process of elimination where I pick and choose the things that I can reduce versus eliminate. It is a constant struggle to remind myself to "chill out" in the smallest of situations. The biggest step was to agree that I was an emotional hoarder and I needed to start organizing this stuff. That meant forgiving.

I recently watched a movie where the topic of forgiveness was at the forefront. The lesson learned is when a person forgives, it has very little to do with those who caused whatever affects you. Forgiveness is for you and your health. You may have to say it a million times, but letting go of some of the hate, anger, and vengeance helped me think clearly. I realized how much energy it took to hate on a daily basis. The first person I had to forgive was the guy I was looking at in my bathroom mirror. I am not sure if he understands what it means yet, but it is beginning to help organize my emotional closet. I can not say I still particularly care for him, but I know he tries to do the right thing. Forgiving, well, we will have to work on that one.

What if I was Gone?

I never have had the thought of harming myself or taking my own life. I have had dear friends do this and I struggle with their decision. I find it difficult to forgive those who take their pain and alleviate it by taking their own life. What that causes are a projection of their pain upon those remaining that loved them. Unfortunately, children fall into that category of pain recipients. The innocence of children is robbed by a loved one's suicide.

I have thought on several occasions, especially in fits of rage, what would everyone's life be like if I were not here? Would it be better, worse, no different? I am not speaking of suicide, I am referring to accident, crime, if we had never met, or perhaps a natural disaster. It is somewhat egotistical to wonder what everyone would do without you. In reality, it is also rather practical to prepare affairs in case something does happen and your family needs to be secure.

I concluded that my wife is a survivor of many things, to include me. She would survive and be successful if I was in her life or not. She also would have been successful if she had never met me. Her level of frustration may be greatly reduced but she did meet me and I am grateful for that.

I think it is important to take a look at oneself and assess the value you provide to those around you. It is not egotistical to take a self-inventory and do a little quality control every now and then. Be a rock, be a lover, be that person that stands with, not on those who love you.

Work

I am fairly certain I would not do well in a large office setting. I have been working from a domicile for nearly seven years. It poses the occasional procedural challenges, but nothing a little creativity cannot overcome. I do not think I could be successful to the level I am now if I'd had a different working environment. Like a warm glove on a cold winter day, this working arrangement at a one-person domicile, fits me. I am the one accountable for everything I do. I like it this way because it is in my control. A larger office setting, or even having one person in my office now, would be like an extended stay at a friend's house. The first night or two would be fun. Play cards, have a few beers, share some laughs. By the third, fourth, or fifth night, you start mentally taking note of the things that the person does that drives you insane. Snoring, loud chewing, slamming doors, anything that is different than the way you live your life. I am certain those same mental notes are being tracked by others as well.

In the day and age of telework and email, technology has been my refuge. I am not required a face to face meeting with anyone unless it is controlled and on my terms. This has been about balance. I can deal with every aspect of my career at an exceptional level. Technology has made this even easier by allowing me to construct reports and requests in digital format.

Rarely would I have to leave the confines of my house. Anything I need to accomplish would be considered structured, planned, and controlled.

Law enforcement is likely the only job that suits me perfectly. We kind of have an understanding after all of these years, me and law enforcement. It tried to kill me a couple of times. I left it because of many reasons a couple of times before. Now, like old high school sweethearts, we are back together again for the long haul. I am very grateful to have the men and women in blue as my coworkers. I also feel very blessed to have this career.

Answer the Question

Let me be clear, I am not a victim. And when I talk about close calls or difficult professional situations, I am well aware that I chose my own career path. I did not choose the situations, but I expected that life was going to have ups and downs. What happened to me was life. From an innocent-minded North Dakota farm kid, to soldier, police officer and Agent, the roller coaster was full of jubilant highs and painful lows. What I was not prepared for was the aftermath and damage that this ride can cause. At the time, it was not discussed nor where there any concrete resources available to help. In a time where understanding or acceptance of stressors was either shamed or not discussed, life-long images, dreams, and other challenges persist. The answer to the question is that all of these symptoms are Post Traumatic Stress Disorder (PTSD).

I have learned that when I have to go into a high stress or high-risk situations, give me the PTSD crew. These are the brave folks that consistently run towards the danger. They have or are willing to sacrifice it all in the name of what they believe. They are made of something very special that would give most people nightmares. They are the fight in "fight or flight". They walk among all of us, watching, waiting to react to protect you, a perfect stranger. They have to survive every day, dedicated to serving those who need protection, whether they like it or not.

PTSD symptoms can creep up on people. Its sufferers are among the strongest in society. It may take years for the symptoms to actually be identified. The important thing to remember if you are suffering with PTSD symptoms is that there are several professionals that dedicate nearly their whole career studying ways to alleviate some of the most aggressive symptoms. PTSD symptoms can cause physical pain, confusion, and affect a person's digestive system amongst other things.

Identification and management of PTSD symptoms had been lacking for years. Some of our heroes from World War II, The Korean War, and Vietnam are just now being diagnosed with PTSD. It has taken a change in the perception of PTSD in order to come up with ways to help those who suffer. Before PTSD was even given a name, there were precursors to it. Common terms often associated with some veterans' symptoms were "Shell Shock" or "Battle Fatigue Syndrome".

My wife and I have had an incredible opportunity to stare directly into the past through a hero's eyes. She has a part-time cleaning business that she does on the side from her other career. One of the clients is a true hero. A World War II veteran who is sharp as a tack. I do not think I have ever met a more kind-hearted human in my entire life. I would take time off to go with my wife while she cleaned his home just so I could hear his stories.

This hero described his time as an 18-year-old, climbing down cargo nets onto waiting water craft on D-day. He said that it became an accepted notion that he and friends would die there and not come back. In some way, that gave him peace. Climbing down the cargo net is what scared him the most. He described how the water thrashed violently against the hull of the ship moving it up and down. The cargo's nets were wet from the splashing water and vomit from those who climbed down before him. His biggest fear was slipping off the cargo net, falling into the water and drowning.

Every story he tells I sit with my mouth open and in absolute amazement. His generation was thrown into unspeakable acts of horror. He sits in his recliner with his walker next to him boldly telling the stories of his life. This amazing hero is one of many that took several walks in hell so that we may live in a country where we can express ourselves without fear of retribution. When we are irresponsible with what has been given to us, we dishonor heroes like this 92 year old veteran and others like him who paid a deep and personal debt for the flag that represents all of us. Technology has changed warfare, but when he lets me see that time through his old eyes, it shakes me to my core. All I can say is, "Thank you Sir".

Times Have Changed

Unlike my wife, I rarely stare at myself in the mirror. I am fairly certain that the passenger side sun visor that conceals a mirror in our vehicle is nearly worn out. In a ten mile trip that visor is up and down probably nine times. I could recommend she just leave it down, but this is one of those little things I just have to let go.

I never really had a reason to peer into a mirror often. I don't have any hair, don't wear makeup, but do occasionally pluck the stray nasal hair that has gone rogue. As I began the process of coming to grips with these symptoms, I forced myself to look at the image in the mirror. A stranger stood before me, staring right back. I really looked into my own eyes. Like our friend the war hero, there was a flood of stories and chaos. No one wants to assess themselves, it's uncomfortable. I had to start listening to my family and wife. I started to listen to the words that come out of my mouth. Some of the crap I would say needed to be addressed in a major way. I needed to be called out on my words and craft them in a way everyone could understand. Worse yet, sometimes I needed to explain myself, which is very difficult for me.

I am here to ask you, to beg you please, if you have ever experienced any of these behaviors, these feelings of isolation, fear, paranoia, anger, frustration at small things in your own life, please speak to someone immediately. If you have changed and don't know why, or feel absolutely nothing any longer, call your peer support.

This is no longer a path untraveled. PTSD and its symptoms do not mean you are weaker, it means you are incredibly strong. You need to learn to manage this strength. My brothers and sisters, if no one answers, call me. I am just a guy learning about all of this, but I do know that the days of shame and embarrassment are over.

The Best and Worst of Humans

Law enforcement officers, regardless of where or for whom you work, are given a different lens in which life presents itself. We are provided a front row seat to the interactions between humans. That interaction is in its most raw and unedited form. We see unlikely heroes saving someone's life. We see people who should be the hero, stand back and not help anyone. I don't know if it comes down to a matter of choice, or just how people are wired.

I recently had the opportunity to volunteer for service where part of our country was devastated by a natural disaster. Because my home town was nearly destroyed by a natural disaster in the past, I found it not only my duty, but also my privilege to help out in any way I could. I have been part of volunteer groups like this before. Typically, there are several "Type A" personalities that clash because everyone's idea is the best. I will say, on this most recent volunteer trip, I witnessed something I had never seen before. I had the privilege to be part of a group that had one focus, helping people and doing whatever it took to accomplish the mission. This rare group produced no drama, arguments, or negative attitudes. That positive attitude projected to the victims and residents of the affected area. I was honored to be part of this group and they are some of the best men and women of which I have ever served.

With every disaster comes those who take advantage of the vulnerable. Disasters provide opportunities for looting, addiction, and other personal crimes that typically occur with more resistance. This is unfortunate collateral damage brought forth by opportunity. That is where law enforcement comes in, attempting to maintain the line of civility and protect our fellow humans. That is really what it is all about for me.

While volunteering for this operation, I met a couple who still had their home, but had been without power. Their love for one another, faith, and attitude put a broad smile on my face. As I sat and drank a cup of hot coffee with them, they shared stories of their over sixty years of marriage. To just sit and listen to these stories made me realize how important relationships between each other really are and are all that matters. Every story that the couple told that day had one specific theme. What got them through each triumph and tragedy was their love and respect for one another. They were so grateful for something as simple as a hot cup of coffee. What they didn't realize was the amazing gift they gave not only to me, but the crowd of police, firefighters, and other emergency personnel that sat down to listen to their story. I am sure I will never see them again, but if they ever read this, I would love to say thank you. I can only hope that I can learn to live, exist, and love the way these two amazing people did.

I don't think law enforcement officers lose that human factor within us. The human factor can easily be misplaced or set aside out of necessity. I do think we sometimes are shocked back into reality when we are up close and personal with multiple victims. The impact we can have on someone's life can either be positive or negative. Often times, that impact is beyond our control. The shear volumes of calls, repetitive nature of certain incidents, and what is going on in our personal lives projects on how we act and perform our duties. To witness the resilience of people, victims, and communities gives hope that there is still greatness in the world. People who are willing to stand up and help one another when it matters most. I witnessed this after the September 11 attacks. Politics, in an instant, became nothing more than a process instead of the main story on the national news.

We Knew it Was Time

We knew it was time. After an episode of complete anger and not caring about anyone or anything in world, we had enough. I was tired of being tired. I was tired of being angry all the time. I hated the thought of other people around me. I was certain that others would certainly take advantage of me or my family if I gave them even a sliver of opportunity. In a brief moment of clarity, I could see that all of my planning and ideas to protect everything was the thing destroying every relationship

I have ever had. I had become a full-time asshole and exceptional part time actor.

We, my wife and I, decided it was time to speak with someone. There are no surprises here. I sat nervously in a waiting room dreading the anticipation of my name being called. My wife was by my side, like she always has been. An energetic man came out and called my name. I should have used a fake name. He offered me a chair in his dark office. Across the small room sat my wife.

I didn't say much that day. I was asked about three questions, and just stopped answering. My wife took over and provided answers to the questions posed by the over energetic man. I felt my face getting red as she described what I had become. Embarrassed, angry, sad, my mouth was dry and my head hurt. Worst of all, my heart broke as I listened to her answer his questions about who I was, what my behavior was like, and worse yet, who I used to be. I felt a hot salty burn slowly travel down my left cheek as I watched my wife's tearful testimony. All that I could do was sit quietly and slowly shake my head. For the first time in a long time, I didn't know what to do.

The man rattled off a bunch of medical terms. His excitement was as if no one had visited him in days. Unfortunately, I was not good company. I wasn't paying much attention. I heard them discussing different scenarios and more questions that would have to be answered. It all seemed like a dream to me. How did I get here? What now? I did know that she was right, and this was the right thing to do.

Thinking in detail about what is really driving you is very hard. What did happen was rather amazing. I started remembering intricate details of some pretty horrible events. When I say details, I mean remembering very insignificant things. These include, smells, stains in clothing, turning on a light switch, or reciting a joke verbatim that was told ten years ago. The mind is an amazing thing, keep it as your ally because it will do what it takes to protect itself and survive.

It Continues

As hard as it is to sit and listen about one's vulnerabilities or faults, it became necessary. The hard work that is done in an attempt to overcome certain horrors never ends. After discussing major issues, working on how to deal with the recurrence of these disturbing memories, and how more are bound to occur, I have learned a lot. The stories and events that I have witnessed will always be with me. They will always affect me.

For instance, I was recently in a horrific car crash. Luckily no one was injured. Being effectively pit maneuvered

by an 18-wheeler at 65 miles per hour is not something anyone
should ever experience. What seemed like five minutes was
clearly a matter of seconds. While being spun around, I recalled
several YouTube videos of officers pit maneuvering dangerous
fleeing felons. I thought, *oh my God, this what a pit maneuver
feels like and it's horrible!*

The anger that followed the terror was so intense that I was
shaking. Incidents like this, if not dealt with, compound on top
of the other stories in our lives. I am grateful we are still here,
but angry that someone, intentionally or not, nearly took
everything we all had. The visions of this incident, like other
incidents, enter my head several times a day. The images my
brain recorded in those seconds visit me in my dreams. It is how
we deal with these compounding memories that is most
important.

I wrote this book because I was a soldier and have been
in and out of law enforcement for 23 years and counting. There
is an important piece of the training puzzle that is completely
lacking for new recruits and veteran emergency services
professionals. We speak of legal ramifications, court cases,
qualified immunity, and other court decisions. We learn to walk,
talk, and act like professionals. We are taught to write reports
from a factual basis. We are trained in so many things, from
vehicle to guns.

We are not taught how to deal with our own stories. We have overlooked one of the most persistent and deadly topics. We are provided resources that have acronyms that we are to reach out and contact should trauma occur within our lives. What we are not taught is that what may be trauma for one person, may not have the same effect on another. We are also not taught that these traumas may not have an immediate effect on our lives.

I am Sorry

There you have it. This is the story of my life thus far. In professional terms, this is my case. The years of not knowing what was happening to me as a human. Looking back, it is very clear how multiple incidents compounded to the point of changing me into the person I have become. The problem was, I didn't even know who that person was. I am sorry that I didn't know sooner. I am sorry to those who had to walk this journey with me. I am sorry I didn't write this book much sooner than now.

We are warriors. Warriors stand, fight, and run to the sound of danger. The point is, we need to take good care of ourselves if we intend to take care of others. It took me until 2018 to learn about and identify these symptoms. 23 years of Law Enforcement and about the only mystery I have not solved is why my wife and family still stand beside me. This will be a constant struggle the rest of my life, but I have found help in my incredibly strong, patient, and forgiving family. For your family, for you, please do the same.

Things that Heal

What has helped me, in more ways than one, is identifying projects and hobbies that help me on a daily basis. Even though work is not a hobby, I enjoy what I do for a living and intensely focus on my tasks.

Music has become my escape. Writing music, playing guitar, and pounding out a beat on one of my drum kits has become nothing but a joy in my life. I would not consider myself an excellent musician by any standard, but as an enthusiast, I am right up there with Beethoven.

Lastly, but certainly not the least, is what you are reading this very moment. Writing these words has helped me beyond my even my own imagination. I encourage anyone to sit down and just start hacking. Writing has always been a close friend to me. I am grateful for the opportunity to be here and share with you my words. I am even more grateful someone took the time to read them. I take the advice of my father who encouraged me to write things down, because someday you will wish you would have. So I did. Thanks Pops!

Of course, there are many more stories I could tell from my twenty-three years in law enforcement. Many more. There were tragedies of such magnitude that before choosing my career, I could not have even imagined. There were frightening, life threating, episodes that still wake me from my sleep and shake me to my core. There are the triumphs of lives saved and the devastation of lives that could not be saved.

I have chosen not to include many of these stories because no matter how I may change the names, towns, and streets, the situations were so unique that the victims, the perpetrators, and perhaps the bystanders could be identified. I do not want the victims to suffer again, so I respectfully keep their stories in the vault of my soul, hoping that life has been kinder to them since our lives intersected.

And while this book consists of my experiences and struggles dealing with humanity and to include my own reactions to those struggles, it is hoped that a larger meaning will be taken from these stories and struggles. The hope is that by reading about my life, others who have had both the opportunity and the misfortune to be responsible for the safety and lives of others, will know that they are not alone should they face the darkness. Also, for those with these awesome responsibilities to know that they are not alone should they question their reactions, and to not bring these burdens to the sanctuary they call home, unable to slough them off. I want them to know there is help out there. It isn't the times when I have been called to action, it has been the time in between that has been intolerable.

I want others to know that in order for self-preservation to occur, it is imperative to seek help when you need it. As you stand fast on whatever color line you represent, protecting the innocent from chaos, be wary that the darkness stands on the other side of the line, staring right back at you.

Acknowledgements

My wife, for guiding me daily and continuing to love me through it all. My son, who can shake his head and forgive like no other. My entire family for taking the time to read what I wrote and still talk to me. I love you all.

My "BETA" for taking a look before I crossed into the unknown: Ruthie Zacher, Troy Schaner, Mary Sue Ohlhauser, Chris Potter, Bob Stanger, Derek "DLB" Breuer, Maggie Masa, Stephen, Jeff Lekatz, Dave, Dr. Norton, Dr. Dahle, Donalee and Fred Strand, and the professionals at the Veteran's Administration in Fargo, North Dakota.

To my beloved "Auntie D", Doreen Rosevold, you are my mentor and inspiration. You encouraged me to write and to continue my projects. There are no words to thank you enough for you guidance, expertise, and friendship.

To my colleagues. Thank you for what you have done and continue to do on a daily basis. Thank you for keeping me and each other safe. Thank you to those who stood beside me in every situation. You are my family.

Dan Hudson and his wife Angie live on a small hobby farm near Detroit Lakes, Minnesota. He is a step-father to Jackson but also to the many of the transient kids that have come and gone from their farm over the years. They share their farm with Willy, a 15 year old Australian Shepard, Mikey, a 12 year old Border Collie/Australian Shepard Cross, and two cats.

Dan has been in public service for 24 years. His passion is helping people through understanding real life experiences. He accomplishes that goal by writing books, poetry, and music. He and Angie are comfortable in most situations, but prefer the quiet solitude of home. Thank you so much for caring enough to read this book. It means the world to all of us.

www.ingramcontent.com/pod-product-compliance
Lightning Source LLC
Chambersburg PA
CBHW061746250726

48657CB00001B/35